Guiding Light

Steadfast to the Son
CYCLE A

Homilies by Fr. Joe Robinson

Shepherds of Christ Publications
P.O. Box 627
China, Indiana 47250 USA

Toll free USA: (888) 211-3041
Tel: (812) 273-8405
Fax: (812) 273-3182
Email: info@sofc.org
http://www.sofc.org

ISBN: 978-1-934222-28-7

Second Printing: 2010

In honor

of our

Beloved Priests

Table of Contents
Cycle A

Foreward

For years all of us have gone to St. Boniface Church in Cincinnati, Ohio. Our family first lived in this parish – Some of the streets named after our relatives –

Fr. Carter was the founder of the Shepherds of Christ Movement and I, Rita Ring, co-founder –

But my brother, Fr. Joseph Robinson was an important part of my life and our lives as we went to his most holy Masses and listened to his homilies as we formed more and more as a body of people producing the Priestly Newsletter and beginning prayer chapters.

God blessed me and all of us being able to go to his Masses and listen to his homilies –

It is a tremendous honor Fr. Joe has allowed us to share these great gifts with you – for greater holiness and knowing more and more about God –

This is the first of a series of these books – dedicated to our priests, out of love for our beloved Church and all the souls of the world.

As you use these great teachings of homilies Sunday after Sunday – please pray the prayers with us as a network of prayer – praying for the priests, the Church and the world –

I thank God every day for the gift of my older brother who has been an important instrument in his priesthood in my life and the lives of all who went to St. Boniface for Mass.

Rita Ring
Co-founder, Shepherds of Christ Movement

Certificate of Marriage

I, the undersigned, do hereby certify, that on the *25* day of *June* A.D. 19*36*

in the church of *St. Boniface* I joined in the

Holy Bonds of Matrimony

William M. Robinson and *Alice Weber*

according to the rites of the Holy Roman Catholic Church.

Henry J. Robinson

Witness: *Marie Weber*

Rev. John H. Schwart

Dedicated to William and Alice Robinson.

Our Mother and Father married on
June 25, 1936 in St. Boniface Church, Cincinnati.

1st Sunday of Advent
December 2, 2007

INTRODUCTION – (Isaiah 2: 1-5, Romans 13: 11-14, Matthew 24: 37-44) The prophet we hear in today's first reading lived over 700 years before Christ. Most probably he had witnessed the destruction of the northern kingdom of Israel by the Assyrians, fierce warriors who came from what is modern day Iraq. The southern kingdom of Israel, centered in Jerusalem, lived in fear and trembling that the same fate awaited them. In spite of great turmoil, his message is a message of peace, a peace we continue to yearn for. It is a peace, however, that flows only from walking in God's ways.

HOMILY – Most of us remember when people used to wait until after Thanksgiving to get ready for Christmas. Now the stores start preparing right after Halloween or earlier. It's interesting that 1500 years ago people in France started preparing for Christmas on November 11 (the feast of St. Martin). They weren't busy shopping, but they prepared by fasting three days a week. A century later Christians were fasting every day from November 11 until Christmas. This was known as "St. Martin's Lent." The practice spread. As far as we know, this may have been the beginning of Advent. Many still remember, I'm sure, that Advent was a time to do penance or give up things to prepare for Jesus' birth. Often we went to confession during that time to prepare ourselves better spiritually. Our world is so different. The aspect of spiritual preparation has slipped into the background, while we busy ourselves with so many other projects that we "have" to finish by December 25. I wonder if those who are trying to get Christ out of Christmas are winning, because in our world today, if Christ plays any part at all in our preparations for his birth, it is only a minor part.

Now, I don't want to sound like "Bah! Humbug!" Joy at Christ's birth is certainly an appropriate emotion at this time. And trying to act kindly to one another and showing greater appreciation for those we love is always in season. But commercialism and materialism has, in so many instances, caused us to shift our focus away from the spiritual side of what we are celebrating.

The real, spiritual meaning of Christ's birth comes only through prayer and reflection. Fasting, as Christians did centuries ago, probably wouldn't do most of us too much harm. Fasting doesn't always involve food. We could fast from smoking, gambling, entertainment, criticizing, keeping so busy that we seldom have time for prayer. Let's not forget the big picture: Christ came down to us for only one reason, to bring us new life, to lift us up to himself. It would be a shame to miss the opportunity Advent offers us to enrich ourselves spiritually and to open ourselves more fully to God's love.

There is another important reason for us to take Advent seriously: being ready to meet Christ when he comes again to call us from this life to himself. Will we be ready? The second reading for today and the gospel stress this aspect of Advent. St. Paul said in today's second reading: "it is the hour now to wake from sleep." And Jesus too tells us "Stay Awake!" We never know when that day will come. Since it's impossible to stay awake physically, it is obvious Jesus is talking about staying awake spiritually. Certainly the people Jesus gives as examples in today's gospel about those eating and drinking, marrying and giving in marriage, those working out in the field or grinding corn at the mill were physically awake, but apparently not all were spiritually awake. They were consumed with their everyday activities and were not prepared when God called them. The examples Jesus uses about two people doing something and one suddenly being taken and the other being left have nothing at all to do with a popular notion known as "the rapture." They emphasize the suddenness with which the Lord may come to any one of us.

Our salvation is nearer than when we first believed, St. Paul tells us. When Christmas comes are we going to celebrate God's love in Jesus' birth or are we just going to celebrate that it's all over? What we do the next few weeks will answer that.

Feast of the Immaculate Conception
December 8, 2007

INTRODUCTION – (Genesis 3: 9-15, 20, Ephesians 1: 3-6, 11-12, Luke 1: 26-38) The feast today is about Mary's conception, that from the instant she began to exist on this earth, indeed from her very conception, she was holy, without sin and filled with God's grace. The gospel today can confuse us somewhat because it tells us about Jesus' conception. It was read, however, because of the greeting the angel used in appearing to her: "Hail, full of grace." Our feast celebrates that there was no moment in Mary's life when there was sin, no moment when God's grace did not fill her.

HOMILY – As we listen in on this conversation between Mary and the Angel, we learn both about Mary and about the child she will give birth to. Mary's child would be Son of the Most High and king forever. He will be called "holy, the Son of God."

This is why Mary was "full of grace," so she could give birth to God's own Son, who would be the source of all holiness. We need to know this, not so that we can put

Jesus and Mary on a pedestal and admire them from afar. Jesus, the holy one of God came to us so that we too can become holy. This is what St. Paul tells us in today's second reading: "God chose us in him to be holy and blameless in his sight."

Most of us do not think of our vocation as a call to holiness. We all want to get to heaven, but most of us think of holiness as reserved for other people, like St. Francis or Mother Teresa. Most of us are content to leave holiness for someone else. We just want to get through heaven's doors. But no one will get to heaven unless they are holy, for holiness means being close to God and sharing God's life. And that's what God's grace does for us: it unites us with God and allows us to share in God's life. If we are in God's grace, then, we are holy people.

Two stories we heard today tell us of our vocation to be holy:

The story in our first reading is about Adam and Eve, our first parents, who originally were very close to God and in their union with God, they were very happy. That was the symbol of the Garden of Eden. But they got greedy! They wanted to be equal to God. The evil one knew how to manipulate them and lead them to ignore God's command. As a result they lost all they had.

The second story in the gospel illustrates Mary's constant attitude of being willing to say "yes" to God, an openness that prepared the way for the Son of God to come to us.

When we were baptized we were filled with God's life, we were born again in God's grace. The very same grace that filled Mary at the moment of her conception, filled us when we were baptized. None of us will ever be as holy as Mary was. She got a head start on all of us.

But if we follow the example of Mary, always ready to say "yes" to God, that will lead us to holiness and to the joy and peace and love that comes with it.

2nd Sunday of Advent
December 9, 2007

INTRODUCTION – (Isaiah 11: 1-10, Romans 15: 4-9, Matthew 3: 1-12) The prophet Isaiah lived during a very troubling time in Israel. During his lifetime the Assyrians annihilated all of the area north of Jerusalem, known as the northern kingdom. Jerusalem lived in fear and trembling that they would be next. Isaiah was not sparing in his condemnation of those who contributed to all that suffering. He condemned not only the Assyrians, but also the kings of Israel who led the people away from God and he condemned the people who followed their lead. In today's first reading he gives hope to those who have remained faithful to God. He promises them God would send them a leader who would lead his people to justice and peace.

HOMILY – A few years ago in my homily I offered this little prayer for people to reflect on. I would like to repeat it for you to think about as you stand in in line at the Post Office, sorting your cards and juggling your packages: "God, our Father, may everything we do be first-class. Imprint your own loving zip code upon our hearts so that we may never go astray. Provide in your gracious Providence special handling for those of us who are fragile and keep us in one piece. And when our days draw to a close and we are marked 'Return to Sender,' be there to greet us at Heaven's door so that no one there might say 'Unknown at this address.' Amen." Too bad we can't tack this up on the post office wall.

We heard Isaiah's promise of a great leader who would lead God's people to justice and peace, a peace that is almost unbelievable. We believe that person is Jesus the Christ. Our readings go on to tell us though, if we want to share in that peace we will not do so unless we follow this great leader and king. And so, lest we get too wound up in all the sending and spending, today's gospel, with its message from John the Baptist, tries to make us aware that more is involved in preparing for the coming of Jesus than sending and spending. Three times in today's gospel John uses the word repent or repentance. When we hear that word we often think of some terrible sinner who needs a total makeover spiritually. If we think this message about repentance does not apply to us, we need to hear again what St. Paul told us in today's second reading: "Whatever was written previously was written for our instruction."

In other words the word "repent" is meant for all of us, not just for bad people. The Greek word for repent in its original meaning meant "to change our mind" As time went on it came to mean "to change our mind to be a different person, indeed, a better person." The prophet John the Baptist is telling us if we haven't been as good as we would like us to be, or as we know God would like us to be, then we need to decide to make a change. Our attitude may need to change or our behavior. Or it could be we're not doing anything too bad, but we're not doing anything really good either. The Baptist said "every tree that does not bear good fruit will be cut down." It's not enough to avoid evil, we have to do good.

It's part of normal conversation around this time to ask "Are you ready for Christmas?" Wouldn't we be surprised if we asked someone that question and they answered: "I still need to do a few things to make myself better spiritually." That kind of an answer would leave us speechless. The media is working overtime telling us how to get ready for Christmas. Let us listen also to John the Baptist, the herald God sent to tell us how He wants us to prepare for His coming. Amen.

3rd Sunday of Advent
December 16, 2007

INTRODUCTION – (Isaiah 35: 1-6a, 10, James 5: 7-10, Matthew 11: 2-11) Today we hear Isaiah speaking to a people in distress, promising them liberation. It is a liberation that will provide fertility for the land (which is mostly desert) and will bring healing for our weakness and our ills. The vision of Isaiah goes beyond any historical distress and anticipates the kingdom of God that the Anointed One, the Messiah, a king who would save his people, would establish. The passage prepares us for the gospel when the disciples of John the Baptist ask Jesus whether he is the Messiah who will establish God's kingdom. Jesus points to his miracles as the answer to their question, miracles that describe the wonderful things Isaiah promises. It began with Jesus but it is a kingdom yet to come which we must wait for patiently St. James tells us.

HOMILY – A man was arrested a couple of weeks before Christmas and brought into court. When the judge asked the man what he was charged with, he answered "doing my Christmas shopping early." The judge replied, "that's not an offense. How early were you doing this shopping?" The man answered, "before the store opened."

That has nothing to do with the today's readings, except that today is Gaudete Sunday, so I thought it would be good to start off the homily with a smile.

In our gospel, John the Baptist was in prison. John got in trouble with the king for condemning the king's immoral life style. While in prison John sent his disciples to Jesus to ask "are you the one who is to come?" In other words, "are you the Messiah, the Savior, the one who is to establish the kingdom of God in our land, or are we still waiting for someone else?" Jesus gave not just a verbal answer but evidence that he was the awaited one. The miracles Jesus worked fit the description of the prophets that he was the one, especially Isaiah whom we heard in today's first reading.

What was the point of John's question? John had leapt with joy within his mother Elizabeth when Mary came to visit. John had pointed Jesus out as the lamb of God who takes away the sin of the world. Why now is he asking: "are you he who is to come?"

There are two possible explanations as to why John asked this question. Prisons in those days were terrible places to be. Perhaps John was feeling pretty discouraged, locked up as he was, possibly contemplating his own execution. John could have been asking in effect, "if you are the Messiah and you've come to establish God's kingdom, where is it?" "If you've come to 'proclaim liberty to captives,' (to quote Isaiah), to set God's people free, what am I doing here in prison?" Was John discouraged, was he losing faith or hope? We really don't know.

Some scholars suggest another reason why John may have sent his disciples to ask that question of Jesus: "are you he who is to come?" Possibly John sent his disciples so they would discover for themselves that Jesus was the Messiah. John had already pointed Jesus out to them, but now he wanted to convince them further. It's a good possibility that was John's purpose.

At any event, whether John's faith was getting weak or whether John was trying to inspire faith in his disciples, we all know how our own faith is challenged when we pray and we try to do good and life beats us down. Why do good people suffer? Why do bad people seem to get by with murder? Life so often seems to be unfair.

There's no one good answer or even a combination of good answers to these questions. St. James gives us one approach to an answer. He tells us we too need to be patient when life seems unfair. God will even things out and those who have been faithful to his word will enjoy happiness beyond our ability to imagine. Patience is especially hard to people in our society today because we have become used to so many conveniences. St. James uses the farmer who has to wait for the harvest as an example of patience. In spite of all the instantaneous conveniences we have in our modern day, there are still things we have to wait for: the birth of a child, for a child to grow up, develop a talent, get a college degree. Patience takes faith, faith that God is at work creating something wonderful, even when I don't see it happening.

Jesus gave us evidence that the kingdom has arrived. But we need patience to wait for its completion. With each 'Our Father' we pray "thy kingdom come." The kingdom of God is still a beautiful promise like the prophecy we heard from Isaiah. Like John in prison, we must keep believing that Jesus is the answer to that promise. He is more than an answer, he is the guarantee of that promise. Through the eyes of faith, we have this guarantee in the Eucharist we now celebrate. "He who is to come," comes to us now. We don't have to look for any other. In this faith we look forward to being able to celebrate his birth once again with the hope his birth gives us and that is our joy at this time. So as our liturgy on this Guadete Sunday tells us: "let us rejoice."

4th Sunday of Advent
December 23, 2007

INTRODUCTION – (Isaiah 7: 10-14, Romans 1: 1-7, Matthew 1: 18-24) – We read almost every day about the problems in the Middle East. This is nothing new. Seven hundred thirty years before Christ there were problems too. The dominant power in the Middle East at that time was Assyria, an especially cruel and powerful nation whose capital was located in modern day Iraq, about 250 miles north of Baghdad. The king in Jerusalem at the time, King Ahaz felt threatened, not so much by Assyria, but by two smaller nations that were preparing to attack him. He decided to call on Assyria for help. The prophet Isaiah, the author of our first reading, warned: "Don't do it. It will only cause more problems." He promised: "God would keep the king and Jerusalem safe." Ahaz did not have enough faith that God would do so. Isaiah told the king "Ask for a sign, ask for some proof." But Ahaz, acting very pious, said he would not tempt God by asking for a sign. Isaiah offered one anyway. The sign Isaiah offered was most probably that God would give him a son who would succeed him. At this time he had no offspring for the king had already offered his only son in human sacrifice to Moloch, the pagan god of the Canaanites. God's gift of another son would definitely be a sign that God would not let his lineage die out. Ahaz' son would be called by the symbolic name Emmanuel for he would be a sign that God was with his people. It is a good possibility that the son Ahaz eventually had was Hezekiah who turned out to be a good leader and a king who was faithful to God. But St. Matthew saw in this promise of Isaiah a greater depth of meaning. He saw that Jesus fulfilled this promise perfectly by being born of a virgin and by being a sign to us that God is with us.

HOMILY – Both St. Matthew and St. Luke tell us about the unique way in which Jesus was conceived. St. Luke tells us the story in the beautiful gospel of the Annunciation where Mary is the central figure. St. Matthew's gospel, which we just heard, tells the story as it was experienced by Joseph.

Joseph learned that Mary, his wife to be, was going to have a baby and he knew he was not the father. It might be worth mentioning that in that culture engagement was as much of a commitment as marriage. That's why sometimes in the gospel it says Joseph and Mary were betrothed and sometimes Mary is called Joseph's wife. It's just that couples didn't begin to live together until they were formally married. We do not know whether Mary told Joseph that it was by the power of the Holy Spirit that she conceived. I would like to think she did. And I would like to think that St. Joseph believed her and decided he was unworthy to be associated with such special people as Mary and her son to be – a son who was conceived by the Holy Spirit. Joseph decided to end their relationship. But if there were any questions Joseph might still have had, the angel made it clear to him. He was to take Mary into his home and he would be head of the family. As head of the family, Joseph would give Jesus his name, a Hebrew name meaning "Yahweh saves." The angel makes a point of this when he tells Joseph "you are to name him Jesus because he will save his people from their sins." It is also Joseph who would give Jesus his social status. That status was indicated by the way the angel greeted Joseph as "Joseph, son of David." Jesus would belong to the house of David, a royal family. Other than the claim to be part of the family tree of King David, the descendants of King David had no power or authority or royal perks since the Babylonian exile 600 years before Christ. But the fact that Jesus had this social standing is very important for the people expected the Messiah to come from David's line as God had promised David his kingdom would endure forever.

On this fourth Sunday of Advent, the Church is reminding us of the exulted dignity of the child whose birth we are about to celebrate. Humanly speaking, he is born into a kingly family. But he is more than human. He was conceived in a unique way, through the Holy Spirit, thus he is Son of God. Truly he is Emmanuel, God with us. He is our God who has come to save us as the name Jesus tells us. No wonder we celebrate.

Let us reflect for a moment on the name Emmanuel. St. Matthew tells us here, in the beginning of his gospel, that Jesus' birth, in the fullest sense of the word, is the fulfillment of the prophecy of Isaiah. Jesus is God with us. If we go to the very end of St. Matthew's gospel, in the very last verse, as Jesus was ascending into heaven, he told his disciples: "Behold, I am with you always, until the end of the age." Jesus is God with us, a theme that begins and ends and runs all through Matthew's gospel.

With all the evil and suffering in our world, it is a mystery why God would want to be with us. Of course, we know from everyday experience we want to be with those we love, so if that's why God wants to be with us, and the gospels tell us that is why, then we ask why God would love us so? We have a hard time believing that God does love us at times, especially when we don't love ourselves very much or when we have to face serious problems or tragedy. At those times we are tempted to feel as if he forgot us. Our only response to times of doubt is to choose to believe him when the tells us: "I am with you always." There's no easy way around the fact that we need to have lots of faith sometimes. There's no easy way to have faith except to take time to pray.

One preeminent sign of his presence with us is the Eucharist. Here too we must choose to believe his words at the Last Supper were true when he said: "This is my body; this is my blood." May our celebration of Christmas truly be a celebration of our belief in Emmanuel, "God is with us." And may it lead us to a greater appreciation of the Eucharist we celebrate each week.

Christmas
December 25, 2007

HOMILY – (Isaiah 9: 1-6, Titus 2: 11-14, Luke 2: 1-14) A tune to shop by: Angels we have heard on high; sing so sweetly while we buy. Demons, too, who lobby hard; for maxing out our credit card.

Christmas is a time when kids tell Santa what they want and adults pay for it. Deficits are when adults tell the government what they want and their kids pay for it.

Christmas – we've heard the story many times, yet it continues to touch our hearts. For children though it is especially moving because they are beginning to get a sense of what it's all about for the very first time. We can look at the statues and let our imagination make it all real for us, the joy at the birth of a child, a very special child, the proclamation of this birth from the angels to the shepherds, the poverty of having to be born in a place where animals were kept and having only a bed of straw to lay on, the love of Joseph and Mary for each other and for this child who came to them and to us as a gift from God.

This year I came across a lengthy poem by Ogden Nash called *The Christmas That Almost Wasn't*. He begins his story telling us about a peaceful kingdom ruled by a wise and gentle king. But he had a nephew who was an evil man. His name just happened to be Evilard. Evilard was an unhappy person and he hated anyone who was happy. Most of all he hated Christmas. One day he gathered some other people just as miserable as he was and he was able to capture the king while the king was taking his nap and he locked the king in the dungeon. Evilard and his gang took over the kingdom and worked to make everyone miserable. One of the first things he did was declare: "There shall be no more Christmas." Evilard decreed: "The man who cries, 'Good Christmas Day!' whall have his gizzard cut away; whoever trims a Christmas tree suspended by the thumbs shall be, and he who sings a jolly carol shall be rolled on spikes inside a barrel…" So spoke the rulers, and grimly smiled thus to destroy one tiny Child, the Christ Child and His Christmas. All the citizens were so upset they couldn't function. Even nature was disturbed. I liked the way Ogden Nash described it: "No one knew when to work, nor yet when to play. For the sun shone by night and the moon shone by day! The mice, they had kittens; the cats, they had puppies; the lions had lambs; and the whales, they had guppies! The ink, it turned white; the mild, it turned black; the pig sang Tweet-tweet, and the cow went Quack-quack. The royal red roses made people to stare, with their flowers in the earth and their roots in the air! The wheat was unground into wheat at the mill, for the river turned round and flowed back up the hill. The spots on the leopard went rolling away and were captured for marbles by urchins at play. Great fires in the towns grew worser and worser; flames put out the firemen instead of vice versa. From headland to mainland, from mainland to isthmus the wide world rebelled 'gainst a world with no Christmas."

I like the way the poems tells us everything in the world was mixed up without Christmas and that's mainly what I want to talk about. Just to complete the poem, however, Christmas was saved by a young shepherd boy with help from St. Wenceslaus. I'm not going to give you the details of how this happened. It would take too long. You'll have to find the book and read it yourself.

The lines of the poem I read tell us the world would be really mixed up if Christ had not been born. We might still be trying to serve hundreds of gods, idols made of gold or silver or wood or stone. We might still be offering people up in human sacrifice to these idols. Would we have ever heard about a loving God, a forgiving God? Would we know that love of God and neighbor are the greatest commandments? Would we have any hope of life after this life, especially risen life? The world would be significantly different, considering over two billion people in the world today believe in Jesus Christ. That's about one third of the world's population. Those who believe in Christ are not perfect. We all sin, we all make mistakes. The peace Christ came to bring us is not here yet. The world is still a better place and we are better people to the extent that we live in his light. Imagine what the world could be if all the different groups of Christians got along with one another and lived Jesus' teachings more seriously. May we continue to live in his grace as we celebrate this great feast of his love. May we look forward to enjoying his love throughout eternity. Amen.

Holy Family
December 30, 2007

HOMILY – (Sirach 3:3-7, 14-17a, Colossians 3:12-21, Matthew 2:13-15, 19-23) Just a few days ago we heard St. Luke describe the birth of Jesus at Bethlehem. Although the manger may not have been the Ritz, we imagined a scene described in the song: Silent night, Holy night. The silence of that night was broken only by the angels praising God and announcing peace to God's people on earth. Now we hear Matthew's gospel. The peace and quiet are gone. The paranoid king, Herod the Great, is intent on destroying the child Jesus and the Holy Family have to escape by leaving their own homeland and becoming refugees in neighboring Egypt. It's like a splash of cold water in the face, but this splash is really a splash of cold reality, reminding us that no family, not even the holiest has a stress-free existence. It also reminds us of the universal conflict and tension between the forces of good and evil, light and darkness, grace and sin. The forces of evil lined up against Jesus right from the beginning. Matthew's story also reminds us that although our decision to follow Jesus takes us along a road that leads to eternal happiness, that road is not always a paved or smooth.

Our focus today is on the family. The importance of the family cannot be overstated or over emphasized. The family is where we discover what it means to be human, what are our strengths and weaknesses, where we experience love and forgiveness, where we learn about relationships, unity, sacrifice, loving others, accepting others, where we learn values and attitudes and trust and how to handle stress and how to be responsible. Family is where we learn how to get along with one another. All these important learning tasks are hopefully learned in a family that is relatively healthy. I say "relatively healthy" because none of us and none of our families are perfect. A family that is seriously dysfunctional teaches a lot of other things that end up not being very helpful. The success of society depends depend on the health of the family. That creates a big burden for families to carry. It also puts a big burden on society to care about the family and to foster healthy families.

Today we celebrate the importance of another family, our parish family. Here too we discover who we are as God's children, how to trust God and to love God and one another. We learn values here too, values that are intended to lead us into eternal life. Hopefully we learn how to give as well as take, how to forgive as well as be forgiven. Here we gather around a family table to be fed, not with perishable food but with food that will nourish us eternally. Our faith community is just as important in its own way as our family of origin. And the Lord's supper that we share is just as important to our spiritual well being as being together and eating together as a family is to our emotional well being.

Today we celebrate 10 years as the united family of St. Boniface and St. Patrick. Back in 1853 St. Aloysius was founded as the Catholic parish in North Side. It didn't last as such. The area grew and there was not always peace between the Irish and the Germans, so in less than 10 years St. Aloysius became two parishes: St. Boniface and St. Patrick. On December 29, 1991 we formally became once again, a single parish. Since St. Boniface was structurally the stronger of the two and since St. Boniface had a school, St. Patrick parishioners moved here and the move was a good one from practically every aspect. Only a hand full of people that I know of were unhappy about the merger. (We passed out a booklet a few years ago which contains much more history about our parish. Most people probably already have one, but if you do not we have some more at the doors of church.)

It has been my privilege to be pastor here for the ten years since our merger. None of us knows what the future holds, but if I could make a guess, I think for many reasons St. Boniface will be here for a long time. As for myself, if my health holds up and if the Archbishop lets me I would like to be here for at least another six years. By then I will be 70. I do not know what I will do when I turn 70. I will have to reevaluate things when I get there.

I do want to say how grateful I am to have so many people's support. There's only one thing I wish, and that is that more people took seriously the serious obligation to attend Mass weekly. I think that for the most part families are strengthened by meals together. And the Lord's supper is our family meal each week. I have seen too many people, once they get away from going to Mass every week, slowly drift away from their faith. St. Paul gives us a wonderful list of virtues that would enhance and enrich any of our relationships with one another, especially the relationships within our families: compassion, kindness, gentleness, humility, patience, forgiveness, etc. Notice in this short passage he tells us twice to be grateful. The words St. Paul wrote of course were Greek, but you might find it instructive to hear what words he used: the verb he used was "Eucharisteo." And he tells us we are to become "Eucharistos." It is obvious from these words that the Eucharist allows us to perfectly fulfill his mandate. It is a perfect act of thanksgiving because, in a special way, we, as God's sons and daughters, offer thanks in union with God' own Son, Jesus Christ. May we, on this anniversary, give thanks for our family in Christ, and for our own immediate families. May we be strong and healthy families, full of thankfulness, and may we rejoice one day in the home of the one Father we all have in common, our Father in heaven. Amen.

Mary Mother of God
January 1, 2008

HOMILY – (Numbers 6:22-27, Galatians 4:4-7, Luke 2:16-21) We have an insatiable appetite for new things. We constantly ask one another "What's new?" The media makes big money keeping us up to date on the latest happenings, good or bad. We read catalogues or search the internet to find out what new things are out there. Some new things are worth celebrating: a new cure for cancer, a new car, a new outfit. Some new things we approach with guarded optimism: a new acquaintance, a new teacher, a new president; and some things are cause for no celebration at all: a new pain somewhere, a new bill we were not expecting.

Most everyone approaches the new year as a something worth celebrating. Perhaps it's as good an excuse for a party as anything else. Perhaps we know our new year's resolutions are going to make us into that kind of person we've always wanted to be. Or perhaps we're just glad we made it this far. There are any number of reasons people celebrate. At the same time, however, if we are realistic, we know each new year could bring new challenges, new dangers, new sadness, new tragedy. These are not things we want to think about and certainly not things to celebrate. They are things to pray about, and that's one good reason to begin the year right here, right where we are now: asking God's blessings for whatever is ahead.

Our first reading today is one that we are all familiar

with as it is often used as our final blessing at Mass. It is a blessing by which Aaron the high priest, the brother of Moses, blessed God's people as they prepared for their journey to the Promised Land. They had been in the desert of Sinai now for a year. God had made a covenant with them and now they have detailed instructions on how to proceed on to the land of Israel, the Promised Land. Their expectations were high as they started out. Unfortunately the journey did not go well. They had the assurance of a close relationship with God, but they easily became dissatisfied with the hardships of their journey. They gave in to fear of what was ahead and complained they would rather be back in Egypt as slaves. The journey they were on required constant trust in God and they found that hard to do. Sometimes God is all we have to rely on.

The difficult moments of our lives call for trust as well. God is taking us on a journey into a new year, into a new chapter in our lives. If we proceed with trust, the journey will go more smoothly. We do have God's blessings on us.

God's blessing is not something we can see. The shepherds saw angels and the baby Jesus. The people of Israel saw miracles after Jesus had grown up. The Apostles saw Jesus after he had risen. We have only a word to depend on, the word of Jesus: "I will be with you always." And we have the special sign of his presence in the Eucharist guaranteed by his word: "This is my body." "This is my blood."

When the shepherds saw Jesus he probably looked pretty much like most any other little baby. They had only the word of the angels to believe he was special. Our host at Mass doesn't look like anything exceptional either, but Jesus' word tells us it is. It is our Lord and our

God who nourishes us as we make our journey through life. This is our guarantee that we have God's blessing on us as we travel on. Having this assurance we who believe can celebrate as we begin a new year. May it be truly blessed for all of us. Amen.

Feast of the Epiphany
January 6, 2008

INTRODUCTION – (Isaiah 60:1-6, Ephesians 3:2-3a, 5-6, Mattew 2:1-12) Jerusalem was destroyed by the Babylonians 587 years before Christ. Fifty years later, the Persians (people living in modern day Iran) conquered the Babylonians, and they allowed the Jews to return home. Their city and their homeland were still in shambles. Rebuilding was extremely difficult. Today's prophet, whom we hear in our first reading, tries to encourage the people and assure them Jerusalem would again be a great city. He sees Jerusalem becoming the center of spirituality and light for all the world. People would come from everywhere to visit Jerusalem and to be nourished by the spiritual light and life radiating from it. St. Matthew sees this vision fulfilled in the birth of Jesus and the coming of the magi. Through Jesus, the message of God's love and salvation will radiate to all the world.

HOMILY – Among the many gods the Romans honored, there was one named Janus. Janus was the god who guarded gates, doors, doorways and hallways. Because doorways are both entry ways and exits, Janus was also considered the god of change and transition, beginnings and endings. He was pictured in art and sculpture as having two heads or two faces, front and back. That was so he could look in two directions, to the past and to the future. The month of January takes its name from Janus as it is the ending of one year and the beginning of a new one. The word janitor also comes from Janus, because janitors have responsibility for locking and unlocking doors and keeping hallways clean.

The feast of the Epiphany comes along at a most fitting time, as it looks back to the past when the prophets tell us that the glory of God shining on Jerusalem would shine out to all the world and would draw people from all nations to walk by its light. It looks to the future when the walls of separation that marked the Jews as God's chosen people and distinct from other nations would tumble, and all people would be invited to be part of and to share in the blessings of God's chosen people.

The coming of the magi symbolizes God's opening a door for all nations, a door that would eventually lead to kings and emperors adoring Jesus as Son of God. This child, who was born in an insignificant part of the Roman Empire, who spent only three years teaching and healing, who died as a condemned criminal, who died with only a handful of followers, in just 300 years would claim three to four million followers and in another 100 years, half the Roman Empire was Christian and Christianity became the official religion of the Roman Empire.

St. Luke told us about the poor, the lowest class of society, shepherds, who initially came to honor the Christ child. St. Matthew tells us of those who were among the elite members of society and their reaction to the birth of Jesus. It is such a contrast in Matthew that those who came to honor the new born Christ were intellectuals, counselors of kings, magi, astrologers and yet they were pagans, while those who had the true faith, King Herod and the religious leaders of the Jews, reacted with paranoia or indifference.

St. Matthew's point is that Christ can now be found

by anyone who seeks him with sincerity and perseverance. The word "Epiphany" comes from a Greek word which means to show, to become apparent, to make an appearance, to illuminate. God has appeared to us in Jesus, or as Jesus says so clearly at the Last Supper, "whoever sees me, sees also the Father." To make himself known, he had to take on human flesh. He did so, so we could know him. The story of the magi shows us that although he has come to us, we have to go part of the way to find him. That is why he gave us prayer and the sacraments. That is why we're here today. May God's Spirit continue to fill us with light so we can continually find him in new and deeper ways.

Baptism of the Lord
January 13, 2008

INTRODUCTION – (Isaiah 42: 1-4, 6-7, Acts 10: 34-38, Matthew 3: 13-17) The words of the prophet Isaiah in today's first reading go back 500 years before Christ. This passage was intended for the Jews who were in exile in Babylon. God is, through the prophet, introducing a person referred to only as God's servant to his people. God is quite pleased with his servant. In a non-violent way, God's servant will establish justice in the world, be a light to the nations and liberation for captives. Scholars debate who this servant might have been 500 years before Christ, but with the coming of Christ, there is no doubt who is God's perfect servant. At Jesus' baptism, God introduces Jesus to the world, not just as his servant, but as his beloved Son with whom he is well-pleased.

HOMILY – If you struggle to understand the baptism of Jesus, you're not alone. Even John the Baptist had difficulty understanding why Jesus came to him for baptism. As John said "I need to be baptized by you, and yet you are coming to me?"

The baptism of Jesus is a mystery worthy of our contemplation. Certainly Pope John Paul considered it as something worth meditating on when he made it one of the mysteries in the new set of mysteries he created for the rosary: the luminous mysteries or the mysteries of light.

Our business manager, Carol Roosa, is taking a course at the Athenaeum to become a parish administrator. She had to present a paper last week and the topic was baptism. The professor was quite impressed with it and so she volunteered to preach this Sunday. I said "no." She said it would only take an hour and fifteen minutes. You would be happy to know I stood my ground. Besides, only priests and deacons are allowed to do a homily. I say all of this to illustrate there is so much that could be said about baptism. I'm not going to say it all. My few words today will, I hope, throw a little light on the sacrament of baptism and might help make the baptism of Jesus a little more understandable.

First I want to point out one way in which the baptism of Jesus by John was totally different from our sacrament of baptism. Then I want to mention one way in which they are similar.

If I were to ask the average Catholic what do you think of when you hear the word baptism, most would answer, "Baptism takes away original sin." That's true but there is a better answer. Let me illustrate. (show wallet) Now many of you know what this is: a wallet. And it's empty, and some of you might relate to that too. That's basically what original sin is. It is emptiness, like this wallet. It's a big nothing. We are empty of God's grace and life. Suppose, for example, by some unbelievable odds, I would win a million dollars in the lottery. I would get that big check (less taxes) and put it in the wallet. If someone were to ask me, "what's in your wallet?," I don't know what I would tell them, but I don't think I would answer "the emptiness in my wallet is gone." But that's what we say when we define baptism as the sacrament that takes away original sin. That definition only emphasizes the emptiness and not the fullness. It doesn't reflect the blessings that suddenly fill us at baptism: the blessings of God's life, of being children of God, the blessings of the Holy Spirit, the blessing of belonging to the family of God, the blessing and hope of sharing in eternal happiness with God. In Jesus there was no emptiness. In him dwells the fullness of the divinity (Col. 2,9) as St. Paul tells us. He was, from all eternity, God's beloved Son. Jesus had no need of baptism in any form. In this respect Jesus' baptism by John made no change in him as the sacrament of baptism did for us. Jesus' baptism by John provides an occasion for us to reflect on our own baptism and the grace that it brought us.

Now I want to describe one way in which Jesus' baptism by John and the sacrament of baptism we received are similar. They are similar in that they are both a commitment. John's baptism was a public commitment people made to live holy lives and to prepare for the coming of God's kingdom. Jesus, in being baptized, was publicly committing himself to do God's will and to preach and build the kingdom of God. Baptism is that for us too. We are committed in a public event to belong to God, to be God's obedient child, God's lover, God's representative. It's something like declaring one's candidacy, not for public office, but for the office of Christian in the world. Most likely someone made that commitment for us, most probably our parents. They made that commitment for us with the intention of directing us in God's ways. Eventually, we have to make that commitment our own if our baptism is going to mean anything at all. On this feast of the baptism of Jesus, we have a good opportunity to recommit ourselves to Jesus. The effects and blessings of baptism remain with us as long as we do not turn our hearts away from the Father who long ago chose us to be his son or daughter in the sacrament. In this way Jesus' baptism by John is very much like our own, not a private, secret event but a public, open declaration of our commitment to love and serve God and others as Jesus, the perfect Son of God did. Amen.

2nd Sunday in Ordinary Time
January 20, 2008

INTRODUCTION – (Isaiah 49: 3, 5-6, 1 Corinthians 1: 1-3, John 1: 29-34) Last week in our first reading we heard about God's servant who would bring justice and light to the world. We hear again about God's servant leading the people of Israel back to God, and bringing God's salvation to the ends of the earth. These passages about God's servant (there are four of them) were written over 500 years before Christ. Scholars do not know exactly who might have fit the description of God's servant at that time, but with the advantage of hindsight we see how perfectly the servant songs describe God's perfect servant, Jesus Christ.

HOMILY – Today I want to talk about gifts and sheep. First gifts. There is no doubt about it, gift giving is a part of us. We just finished a very busy time of gift giving and already the stores have put out things for

Valentine's Day. Sometimes gifts are not sincere, they are given with strings attached or because they are expected or to gain someone's favor. But most of us give gifts to one another simply out of appreciation or gratitude or love.

Just as much as it is a part of our nature to give gifts to one another, it has always been basic to human nature to offer gifts to God. I would like to think most of the time our offering to God comes from appreciation or gratitude or love, and it probably does, but in the back of our minds we're also hoping to win a few points with God. That's okay. God understands and appreciates hearing from us even when it's for our own self-interest. Didn't he teach us to ask for the things we need.

When we give a gift to God, it is called sacrifice. All ancient religions that I know of had some form of sacrifice, which indicates to me that sacrifice is instinctual. Some primitive religions offered human sacrifice, the implication being that human life was the most precious gift they had to offer. In the story of Abraham's readiness to sacrifice his son Isaac, God revealed to the Jewish people this was not what he wanted. The Israelites offered food and drink which symbolized their life. Without food and drink we die, so in the offering it was their way of saying they recognized they owed their life to God. Grain and wine and oil were offered, but the primary offering was an animal (when they had the means to afford it), most frequently a lamb. Thus my second theme: sheep. Other than seeing lamb on a restaurant menu occasionally, or counting sheep when we turn in for the night, the thought of a lamb seldom crosses our mind. But sheep were, and still are in the Middle East, as common as cell phones are in our culture today. They provided wool for clothing, meat for festive occasions, and sacrifices for their God. In the Temple of Jerusalem, priests offered a lamb twice a day as a sacrifice. At the time of Jesus, on the Preparation Day before Passover, the Jewish historian Josephus tells us over 250,000 lambs were sacrificed for the traditional Passover meal. Although this number could be an exaggeration, Josephus is telling us the priests were kept mighty busy on that day. The sacrifice of the paschal lamb took place only in Jerusalem, beginning at noon. This was the same time Jesus was condemned and died on the cross. St. John, in his gospel, specifically connects Jesus' sacrifice with the sacrifice of the paschal lambs when he tells us that when Jesus was pierced with a lance it fulfilled the Scripture, which said "not one of his bones shall be broken." That was a requirement for the Paschal lamb. (Jn 19,36)

Jesus' sacrifice of his life was offered in perfect obedience and love and fidelity to his Father and to the mission his Father gave him. Because it was the sacrifice of the Son of God it had infinite value. Because of its infinite value, it made all other sacrifices obsolete. Moreover, Jesus made it possible for all of us to share in this perfect sacrifice to the Father when at the Last Supper he said the words: "do this in memory of me." To digress for a moment: Somehow in this day and age, it seems the more we have been blessed, the more we take for granted and the less grateful we have become. I sense that many people these days think of God as some kind of rich uncle who is there to give them what they want. When he doesn't do so, they just turn their backs and sort of say: why waste time on someone who won't do what I want them to do.

Back to the gospel. Could John the Baptist have any of this in mind about Jesus as the perfect sacrifice when he called Jesus the "lamb of God?" Certainly John recognized the saving mission of Jesus for he refers to

Jesus as the one who would take away the sin of the world. I hope it doesn't complicate things too much if I say the following: In the Greek John uses the words: "lamb of God." Scholars have gone back to the Aramaic which is what Jesus and the Baptist would have spoken most of the time and they tell us the Aramaic word for "lamb" was *talya*, which also meant "servant." Thus we see the title "Lamb of God" connected with the first reading about God's servant who would be a light to the nations that God's salvation might reach to the ends of the earth.

I want to conclude by making one last reference to the term "Lamb of God." Here we can look at the Book of Revelation (a.k.a. the Apocalypse). Jesus is represented there also as a lamb, a lamb who was slain, but who is now enthroned and glorified, praised and worshipped by all the heavenly hosts. From the throne of God and from the lamb flows life and blessings of every kind. Those who will enjoy these blessings and who will share in his victory are those who have followed the lamb. The Lamb of God is not just a perfect gift to God, but the way to eternal life for all of us. As we offer our perfect gift to God through Jesus our paschal lamb and worthy servant, may it help us be more faithful and grateful servants of our God.

3rd Sunday in Ordinary Time
January 27, 2008

INTRODUCTION – (Isaiah 8: 23 – 9:3, 1 Corinthians 1: 10-13, 17, Matthew 4: 12-23) Galilee is located about 75 miles north of Jerusalem. With cars and expressways, that doesn't seem very far today, but since most people traveled on foot at the time of Jesus, it was a considerable distance. Galilee had a difficult history. Seven hundred years before Christ the Assyrians destroyed Galilee and took most of its citizens, the ones they didn't kill, and moved them far away from their homes in Galilee. That kept conquered nations from regrouping and rebelling against them. A lot of pagans were moved into Galilee. By the time of Jesus seven hundred years later, there were still a lot of pagans living there and Jews as well who had moved back so the population was pretty well mixed.

In spite of its destruction by the Assyrians, and the devastation they left behind, the prophet Isaiah, who was at that time living in Jerusalem, foresaw good things for Galilee. Into the spiritual and social darkness that covered the land, Isaiah said a light would shine. You might remember those lines from the first reading on Christmas. St. Matthew quotes this long passage from Isaiah to tell us Jesus was the fulfillment of that prophecy. It would have been normal for a religious teacher like Jesus to do his preaching and teaching mainly in Jerusalem. (Joachim Jeremias pg 242) Jesus however chose to begin his ministry in Galilee where he spent most of his life. Jesus was the light that the people of Galilee, the people living in darkness, had longed for. In these readings Galilee is called by the names of two of the tribes of Israel that originally settled there: Zebulun and Naphtali.

HOMILY – According to the Bible, the first gift God created was light. Afterwards, when God was creating other things like fish and birds and cattle and creeping things and animals and human beings he gave us all eyes to be able to appreciate what the light revealed to us. And he gave us a brain to be able to interpret, to a greater or lesser degree, what is seen. Although we wonder at times how intelligent human beings are, science tells us we humans have the most developed brain of all life on this planet.

With our imaginative and creative and logical minds we can see things that do not even exist, including abstract ideas. We speak in terms of light and seeing when we have ideas, such as: "I see how that's done," or "this just dawned on me," or "I saw the light." This notion of seeing something with our mind's eye also applies to spiritual things too. St. Matthew describes Jesus' ministry in Galilee in the words of the prophet Isaiah: "the people who sit in darkness have seen a great light." Jesus spoke of light to describe his own ministry when he said: "I am the light of the world. Whoever follows me will not walk in darkness, but will have the light of life." (Jn 8,12) The term "revelation" is a theological term that identifies this light that God gives us. When we let ourselves be guided by that light it is called "faith." Faith is nothing other than a way of seeing with God's own eyes. Our faith gives us a vision that ironically comes, not through what we see with our eyes or create with our minds, but through what we hear with our ears! It tells us why we were created, how we are to live, how we are to treat one another, what is going to happen after we die. It is a vision that is sometimes crystal clear, like when Jesus tells us about the importance of love for God and for each other. Other times it is blurry; for example, when St. Paul talks about the next life, he tells us "at present we see indistinctly, as in a mirror" (mirrors were not so wonderful in those days.) Faith is a way of seeing that is based simply on the word Jesus spoke to us. In some cases, what we see in faith contradicts what we see with our eyes, like: "This is my body." It contradicts what we see, but in faith we choose not to believe our eyes but to believe God's word which we have considered to be more reliable. I wonder how much brighter life would be for all of us and for the world in general if our minds and hearts were more open to the light that Christ has brought us.

When we were baptized a candle was given to us with the words, "Receive the light of Christ." For most of us that candle was given to our parents or sponsors to hold for us. It was up to them to help us live by that light. Obviously we have lived by that light or we wouldn't be here today. I commend you for that and thank you for it.

But that light should not be kept hidden. Through confirmation we have been commissioned to bring that light to others. Jesus not only said "I am the light of the world, but he also said "you are the light of the world." Today we heard about Jesus choosing four disciples who would one day set the world on fire with his light. But they did their job a long time ago and passed Christ's light on to others, and those others passed it on to others and eventually it got to us. We have the faith because someone led us to it. If others in the future are to have the faith, it will depend on us. We have to share with others the light we have received. We don't have to get up and preach to do that. We can do it by the way we live, by being morally good, honest, loving people. We can invite people to come to church with us. When we have the opportunity, we can share our faith by simply telling others what our faith means to us. When we try to debate doctrine, we can get in a big argument, but if we tell someone how much my faith means to us, who can argue with that?

In summary, God has blessed us in many ways. One of the reasons we're here today is to give thanks (that's what Eucharist means). He created light and gave us the ability to see by it. But God gave us the greatest gift of all when he sent his Son, Jesus, to us and gave us the ability to believe in him. For his light will enlighten our lives throughout eternity. May others come to walk in his light too. Amen.

4th Sunday in Ordinary Time
February 3, 2008

HOMILY – (Zephaniah 2:3; 3:12-13, 1 Corinthians 1: 26-31, Matthew 5: 1-12a) Imagine a drug that causes you to live eight or nine years longer, make $15,000 more a year and be less likely to get divorced. "Happiness seems to be that drug," according to Martin Seligman a PhD psychologist who researches and writes about happiness. If we're miserable, can we make up our mind just to be happy as easily as if we were to take a pill? To some extent we can. Studies on twins say that about 50% of our happy or unhappy moods is genetic. About 10% depends on depressing life circumstances such as being extremely poor, gravely ill or losing a loved one. The other 40% we can control and is influenced by what we do to make ourselves happy. We just have to be careful not to pin our hopes for happiness on things like perfect health, lots of money, and good looks, which bring only a tad greater happiness than those less blessed. True happiness flows from deeper values such as engagement with family, work or a passionate pursuit, and finding meaning from some higher purpose. Does that sound like getting out of ourselves? Sitting around feeling sorry for ourselves just won't do it.

Four ideas that I think are very helpful for increasing happiness are (1) Being active (such as exercise) or (2) putting on a happy face. I think when we smile or laugh it tricks our mind into thinking we're happy and we feel happier. (3) I've always preached that gratitude is the key to happiness. Psychologists are suggesting that people keep a gratitude journal, writing down at the end of the day the things that happened that cheered them up. Experts say counting your blessings may be the single most helpful thing you can do for you happiness. (4) Doing good things for others can help too.

There are those times when a person needs professional help and/or medicine. There is that 50% that is genetic where some types of depression seems to be inherited or that 10% when a person is in a seriously difficult place in life. Self medication with alcohol or other forms of addiction only add to the problem. If you need the help, get it. There's no shame in that. A lot of depression is due to internal chemistry or external circumstances which a person can't handle on their own. For many of us the attitude we have toward life (seeing the glass as half full instead of half empty), the attitude of gratitude, of helping others, of getting out of ourselves, of surrounding ourselves with cheerful people or positive thoughts can help improve our own happiness quotient.

Then there's our faith which gives us hope. Jesus gives us the beatitudes, which form the introduction to his sermon on the mount. His sermon is three chapters long, by the way, which we will totally miss. We'll hear the very last part in June after the Lent and Easter cycle. Jesus is talking to the common people of his day, people who were living close to the edge, people under the rule of Rome, people surviving day to day. He is letting them know life's troubles and difficulties will some day be reversed for those who open their hearts to the Kingdom he came to announce. The Greek word (and Greek is the language in which we find the original form of the gospel we have) the Greek word that begins each beatitude is "μακάριος." The word means "happy" in an ordinary sense, but it also means one who is especially happy or favored or fortunate. That's why it is translated "blessed."

Reflecting on the beatitudes, it makes perfect sense to me to say that those who are poor in spirit, i.e., who are satisfied with simple things in life, those who are merciful, those who are clean of heart will be happy or blessed. It wouldn't make much sense at all to say "happy" or "blessed" are those who mourn, those who hunger or thirst for righteousness, those who are persecuted unless somehow God would remove their sadness and let them share in his joy. In that lies our faith and hope. The thing that keeps me going is to keep believing that God can bring something good out of everything. Without the happiness and hope that thought gives me, I would have given up in despair many times. Similarly I have often heard the Archbishop say during difficult times: "God's in this somewhere." I don't always see how God can make things better; I just believe he can. That's because I believe in the resurrection. If God could turn Good Friday into Easter Sunday, he can turn our sadness, our losses, our crises, our sicknesses into a blessing for us. That is the hope God gives us.

The Holy Father just finished his second encyclical: On Christian Hope. He says: our great hope – faith in Jesus – can sustain people during the roughest of times. He goes on: we need God otherwise we remain without hope. That's what brings us to Mass every week. We celebrate Jesus' death and resurrection, his body given for us and to us, and his resurrection that gives us hope that even death cannot defeat us if we stay in union with him. Blessed are we who believe in him and blessed are you for being here today. Amen.

5th Sunday in Ordinary Time
February 6, 2005

INTRODUCTION – (Isaiah 58:7-10, 1 Corinthians 2:1-5, Matthew 5:13-16) Ancient Babylon was in modern day Iraq, with its capital on the Euphrates River, less than 100 miles south of Baghdad. When the Babylonians conquered the Jews in 587 BC, they took most of the Jews off to Babylon as prisoners and slaves. This event, known as the Babylonian exile, lasted 50 years. When the Persians, people who lived in modern day Iran, conquered the Babylonians, the Persians allowed the Jews to return home. Most of those Jews who returned to Israel were the grandchildren of the ones who were taken into exile. When they got home to Israel, they found their cities and farms in the same deplorable state in which they had left them when they were originally conquered 50 years earlier. They had to rebuild everything, their farms, their homes, their businesses, their cities, their temple. And here is where our first reading comes in. Their efforts to survive created deep division in the community. It was survival of the fittest, and the poor and homeless were ignored. God is telling them that their selfish, self-centered, 'every man for himself' attitude was not going to be successful. If they wanted to grow and thrive, they had to start caring about each other. Justice, fairness, honesty and kindness would bring light into their darkness. Selfishness would bring continued suffering.

HOMILY – The words of Isaiah are as true now as they were 2500 years ago. We can make our world beautiful by the way we treat each other or we can make it a very unpleasant place to be. If everyone's only concern is about themselves, the survival of the fittest, few will survive and not very happily. If we work together, we will do more than survive, we will thrive. As Ben Franklin said at the signing of the Declaration of Independence: "We must all hang together, or assuredly we shall all hang separately." And Jesus, as he continues the Sermon on the Mount, tells us "you can do it." "You are the salt of the earth. You are the light of the world." When we think of salt, we think of how it makes our food taste better, but we better not eat too much of it. It's a pretty cheap item in our world today, but at the time of Jesus it was a very valuable commodity. So valuable in fact that the word "salary" comes from the Latin word for salt: "sal." In those days it not only made food more tasty, but it was used very much like we use refrigeration today: as a preservative. There is no need to emphasize the importance of light on our world today as well as at the time of Jesus. Don't forget Jesus was talking to a large group of people, not just his picked Apostles. He was talking to fishermen, farmers, housewives, merchants, carpenters and stonemasons, old people and young. He told them: "You are the salt of the earth, you are the light of the world." God has given us the ability to bring light and joy to others in simple ways as well as in major ways.

I came across an interesting story to illustrate this. It is the story Art Linkletter tells about himself. He was the child of an unwed mother who gave him up for adoption. (It's a good thing he was born in 1912 rather than after 1973 when abortions became legal.) His adopting parents were warm and loving, but not very good providers. His father tried several careers, including preaching, and was a financial failure in each of them. At the tender age of 16, Art left home and hit the road as a hobo. Instead of finding his fortune as he set out to do, he almost got killed. A couple of tough guys found him and a buddy sleeping in a boxcar and robbed them. They almost shot them, but at the last minute thought differently about it. Instead, one of the guys who robbed him took pity on him and gave him back 30 cents out of the $1.30 he stole from him. He thought Art might need to have something so he could buy himself some breakfast. His first job was sorting through discarded lemons from a fruit-packing plant, picking out the least rotten fruit and selling it door to door. Somewhere between that difficult start and today, Art became the star of two of the longest-running shows in broadcasting history, he became a successful businessman, author and lecturer. He was married to the same wife, had five children, seven grandchildren and 80 great grand children. He tells his story to encourage others who are at the lower rung of the economic ladder, who think they have few gifts or talents they can offer others. He said, "if I could do it, you can too." Jesus says: "you are the salt of the earth, you are the light of the world." Amen.

6th Sunday in Ordinary Time
February 11, 1996

HOMILY – (Sirach 15:16-21, 1 Corinthians 2:6-10, Matthew 5:17-37) Doctors and nutritionists have been telling us for years that what we feed our bodies is going to affect our health. Likewise many wise and intelligent people have also been telling us that what we feed our minds is going to affect us in many ways, physically, emotionally and socially. There are those, however, who do not agree. For example, a number of groups are upset that the new telecommunication bill that was passed this week outlaws the transmission of sexually explicit and other indecent materials to minors over computer networks. Apparently they think kids (and adults too) can feed their minds with all kinds of garbage, without any ill effects. These people must not be aware of the fact that our society is seriously being weakened and harmed by promiscuity, divorces, sex crimes, abortions and illegitimate births. But despite the efforts of civil libertarians to protect our freedom to feed our minds on whatever unhealthy or toxic diet we choose to, scientific research continues to demonstrate what is obvious to most common sense people that there is a connection between what shapes our thinking and how we behave. Just this week a study has come out proving that viewing violence on TV or in movies definitely encourages aggressive and violent behavior in the viewer. This is especially true when violence is shown in such a way that criminal violence goes unpunished or is even rewarded, or it is shown without also showing the human suffering that results from such violence.

I think that what I am saying connects with what Jesus tells us in today's gospel. Our emotional, moral and social health begins with what's in our mind. And so he tells us not only is murder wrong, but so is the mental attitude of hatred and unforgiveness that we may choose to carry around within us. Even if we never act it out by killing someone, an attitude of hatred and revenge will affect not only the person who holds on to such feelings but also his or her relationships with others. The same is true with regard to sexuality, honesty and so on. Now, I am not talking about those passing temptations that we all have, where we may feel extremely angry toward someone, or we feel a surge of physical attraction toward someone. I am talking about holding on to those feelings, nurturing them, wanting to keep them. Our first reading says that before us is life and death, whichever we choose we will have. Choosing to hold on to negative, destructive, sinful, or evil thoughts will only bring those kinds of results.

There is an area of psychology, I called cognitive therapy. Cognitive therapy is a form of therapy that helps people deal with a certain emotional problems. The approach it begins with is to help people control their thoughts. For example, how can we be happy, how can our mood be bright if we are always thinking negative, depressing, gloomy thoughts. What we feed our mind, not just on TV or the Internet, but especially what we feed our mind by the things we say to ourselves, can affect not only the way we behave, but the way we feel. I am 100% convinced that this is true, because I experienced it myself when I was younger. I was always going around condemning myself and putting myself down, and then I couldn't figure out why I was depressed. Once I became aware of what I was thinking and started to change my thoughts to ways of thinking that were healthier and more fair to myself, my mood changed too, for the better.

I would like to conclude by offering another example. Thoughts are like seeds we put in the ground. The kind of seeds we put in will determine the kind of plant that grows. The kind of thoughts we plant in our minds, or that we let others plant there, will affect our attitude, our mood and our behavior. This is why it is so important to read good literature, to support worthwhile programs, to pray and to reflect on God's word and to meditate. Our Lord is telling us we have to have control over our thoughts, we have to make good choices about what we feed our minds, because, for better or for worse, our thoughts are going to control us.

7th Sunday in Ordinary Time
February 18, 1996

HOMILY – (Leviticus 19:1-2, 17-18, 1 Corinthians 3:16-23, Matthew 5:38-48) We are in the section of St. Matthew's gospel that is called the Sermon on the Mount. This sermon goes on for a full three chapters and covers a whole variety of topics. There is in Israel today the Church of the Sermon on the Mount. It is built at the top of a gently sloping hill, just about three miles from Capernaum, where you can get a beautiful view of the Sea of Galilee and all the surrounding area. The image that St. Matthew is trying to convey as he pictures Jesus preaching on this hill, is to present Jesus as a new Moses giving us God's new law. Just as Moses came down from Mt. Sinai and proclaimed the Commandments, so Jesus is now the new lawgiver, not abolishing the law as he says, but perfecting it.

Last week we heard in the gospel more specifically what Jesus meant when he said he came to perfect the law. In reference to the fifth commandment, "thou shall not kill," he taught us we should not even be harboring hateful and murderous thoughts and desires within ourselves. In a similar way he spoke about the sixth commandment, "thou shall not commit adultery." Today's gospel continues this pattern. The law of talion, which Jesus refers to today, an eye for an eye and a tooth for a tooth was meant to impose some sense of justice and fairness. A person could exact revenge only to the extent of the damage imposed. In other words, if someone knocked out one of your teeth, you could only knock out one of theirs, not three or four, in retaliation. Jesus carries the law much further, in telling us not to try to take revenge at all. He insists that love has to go beyond what is demanded, it has to go beyond just loving people we are supposed to love or enjoy loving. It's not easy to do but we have his example to show us how it can be done.

Whenever I hear the passage about going the extra mile I always remember my aunt. It was one of her favorite passages. You might remember at the time of Jesus the Romans government ruled the Jewish people and by law a Roman soldier had the right to make a Jew lead him somewhere or make him carry something for him for a mile, but he could not make him go further. Jesus said do more than you have to. "Should anyone press you into service for one mile, go with him two miles." My aunt Dorothy lived by this principle. She was always ready to go the extra mile for people, always ready to do more than what she had to in the community or in her job at the public library. Of course following Jesus advice not only helped her to be a better Christian, she also became very successful in her work and much respected and appreciated because she was the way she was.

Jesus sums up this section by saying you must be perfected as your heavenly Father is perfect. It is impossible for any of us, as wonderful as we may be, to be as perfect as God is, and if we think we should be, we will just add a great deal of neurosis to all our problems. What Jesus is asking of us is that we should all be trying to get closer to God, by our relationship with God and by our love for one another. That is the same thing that Moses is saying in the first reading "be holy, for I the Lord your God am holy". Someone told me the other day, to be perfect is to be in process. In other words, we are perfect when we keep growing, we keep maturing, we keep moving forward in God's direction. When we stop moving forward spiritually, when we decide to put God off to some time when we're 'not so busy', when we say for example, there's nothing special I need to do for Lent, there's no way I need to change for the better, or it's not worth the effort, then we become stagnant spiritually. And that's bad. For the development of our spiritual life is our most important purpose in life. Our material possessions we will leave behind some day. Our bodies will decompose. The only thing we will have that we will be able to hold on to when this life is over is the good works we have done and the relationship with God we have formed.

We want to be like God in possessing some of God's qualities: like joy, love, peace, eternal life. We have to work to be like God in other ways, especially in our everyday lives and our everyday dealings with one another. And the only way to get started in this direction is through prayer. We need to reflect on God's word, we have to provide for ourselves moments of quiet where we can possibly hear God speak in our hearts. Thomas Merton in a little book on contemplation says "there are so many Christians who do not appreciate the magnificent dignity of their vocation to sanctity, to the knowledge, love and service of God. There are so many Christians who do not realize what possibilities God has placed in the life of Christian perfection – what possibilities for joy in the knowledge and love of Him. There are so many Christians who have practically no idea of the immense love of God for them, and of the power of that Love to do them good, to bring them happiness." If you are looking for something special to do during Lent, if your life is in such perfect order in every way and you can't think of anything you can do to make it better, I would suggest taking some extra time to pray.

8th Sunday in Ordinary Time
February 25, 1990

HOMILY – (Isaiah 49:14-15, 1 Corinthians 4:1-5, Matthew 6:24-34) I'm sure at Jesus' time, there was a lot of stress and anxiety. Israel was a country ruled and taxed by an oppressive foreign power. When they said, "what to eat . . ." their main concern was IF they would have anything to eat.

I don't know whether their anxiety was greater or less than what we have to face – broken homes, aging parents, delinquency, drugs, AIDS, nuclear weapons, etc. I do know this: even though we have Maalox and martinis, tranquilizers and psychology, we still need to hear the Lord's wisdom in today's gospel.

The American Academy of Family Physicians estimates 2/3 of office visits are prompted by stress-related symptoms. These include shortness of breath, dizziness, palpitations, trembling, sweating, feeling of choking, nausea, numbness, fear of dying or going crazy, muscle tenseness, inability to concentrate, not sleeping or sleeping too much, not eating or eating too much. Beyond this, stress is a major contributor, either directly or indirectly, to coronary heart disease, cancer, lung ailments, accidental injuries, cirrhosis of the liver, and suicide.

Many things relate to how stress affects us: exercise, diet, quality of our relationships, the nature of the stressor (the event or the person causing us stress). One thing especially is related to how well we cope with stress: the meaning or interpretation we put on the stressor. To what degree and to what extent do we see it or interpret it as something threatening to us? One example, among thousands, is criticism. Some people have the type of personality that is always insecure. They see everything as threatening. We call them worriers. They worry even if they don't have something to worry about. Psychologically, they might be said to have a personality trait that is characterized by high anxiety. As Jesus said, they might be weak in faith, or they might have some other emotional predisposition that causes their worrying. For instance, they might have grown up in a home where they felt no security.

I work professionally with people who suffer emotional pain. Sometimes strengthening one's faith is a real help. Sometimes counseling or behavioral modification is helpful. Often it is a combination of methods. For many of our ordinary, everyday stresses and anxieties, the Lord's words can be a real strength and can keep them from getting worse. He is telling us our God loves us. We belong to God, so "enough of worrying."

Jesus, our Savior, promises us a future – heaven or hell. But he also came to save us right now. Healing people, sending disciples to heal. He came to bring us life in its fullness. These words of wisdom can save us from many of our anxieties and fears as well as be a source of healing. Enough of worrying; let that be our prescription for health.

Jesus was not telling us to be irresponsible. We have to work to provide for ourselves and family. We have to study to pass exams. We have to make efforts to develop and improve. Remember the story of the talents. Jesus is not telling us we should stop earning a living, but he did tell us we cannot give ourselves to God and money. Here money symbolizes all those things that can make us self-centered and not concerned about God and others.

When we think we can get along well without the Lord, we really are setting ourselves up for stress and anxiety because then we are programming ourselves to think we have to make it on our own. We must realize we can't do it. We have a God who helps us – a God who is our rock, our salvation, our stronghold – from him comes all our hope.

9th Sunday in Ordinary Time
March 4, 1984

HOMILY – (Deuteronomy 11:18, 26-28, 32, Romans 3:21-25, 28, Matthew 7:21-27) Most of us think of Jesus as kind, sympathetic, loving, understanding, merciful, forgiving, gentle, meek, our friend, our brother, our helper. He is all of these and we like it that way. At times, however, because he is loving and caring, he has some strong things to say, things to shake us out of our apathy, our routine, our comfort level, and our complacency. I think today's reading is one of those hard sayings.

It is hard because we don't like to hear that we might fail. Jesus tells us we either build our house on rock or we build our house on sand. There are no in-between situations. We can either build our life on him and we have stability, strength, and endurance, and we will survive. Or we can choose not to build our life on him. No matter what form that takes, no matter what we build on lives on, it is sand. It won't support us for long; it won't last; it will leave us in ruins. There is no in-between ground. There is only rock or sand. There is obeying and following his word or not obeying and following it. This kind, sympathetic, loving, understanding, merciful, forgiving Lord tells us we have only two choices – one that leads to life – one that leads to ruin. There are no compromises.

When I work as a counselor, one of the things I try to be sensitive to is the value of compromise. A husband wants things his way; his wife wants it another. You try to figure out how they can both be satisfied, how they can compromise.

Here, however, there is no compromise between hearing the Lord's words and obeying them or turning a deaf ear to them. We can't obey them partway; we can't obey what suits us and ignore the rest. This is common today. People say, "I believe in God, but I don't have to go to church," or "I don't do anything to hurt people" (although I may not be doing anything to help people either), or "I know what the Lord says about this or that, but he won't mind if I behave differently; he understands." Or just as bad: " I don't know what the Lord says about this, but I feel like it's all right." For some people religion can be a lot of talk and nothing else.

We can go through life saying, "Lord, Lord" but not doing the will of the Father. Saying "I believe in God" but not doing anything about it means nothing. Even if we could work miracles and cast out demons in his name, our life is built on sand if we do not hear this word and put it into practice.

The Lord's words sound hard and they are, but they come from a loving, kind, sympathetic Lord who died to save us. He doesn't want to see us lost. [This Wednesday begins the season of Lent. For some people it means little more than getting ashes on Ash Wednesday and palms on Palm Sunday. If we take this time of year seriously, the Church calls us into a time of self-examination – a time of scrutiny, a time to help us identify in our lives those compromises we slip into. It is a time of conversion and change (for the better), a time to make up for past failures and begin again; a time of more intense prayer, a time to hear God's word and to try to a greater degree to build our lives upon it. We can make this season a time of renewal for ourselves and our family, or we can get through it without allowing any kind of spiritual change to disrupt us and our daily routine.

Our ashes this Wednesday remind us that there is nothing imperishable, nothing immortal, nothing eternal except God and the new life he gives us through his Son Jesus.

As Jesus tells us today, there is nothing we can build our lives on that will bring us this eternal life except to obey his word. This is the rock to build our life on; everything else is sand.

1st Sunday of Lent
February 10, 2008

INTRODUCTION – (Genesis 2:7-9; 3:1-7, Romans 5: 12-19, Matthew 4: 1-11) Today's first reading tells us the story of the creation of our first parents, their temptation and their fall from grace. This does not pretend to be a documentary of what happened one or two million years earlier. It is more like a parable that attempts to understand the problem of evil. God created the human race to be happy and to share in his grace and friendship. This is indicated by the Garden of Eden. This story of Adam and Eve tells us the source of evil is our decision to give in to temptation, to not trust, to make our own rules, to use the free will which God gave us to say "no" to God. The story shows us that we bring suffering upon ourselves as a result. Paul, in the second reading, reflects on this sinful tendency in all of us. But his emphasis is on the good news that Christ can save us from sin.

HOMILY – A teacher asked her little children in religion class to draw a picture of their favorite bible story. One small boy drew the picture of an elderly gentleman, elegantly dressed, driving a big convertible. In the back of the car were two people, hardly dressed at all. The teacher thought it was an interesting picture and asked what it meant. The young artist was surprised the teacher had to ask, but he explained that was God driving Adam and Eve out of the Garden of Eden.

Today's gospel, where Jesus refuses to give in to temptation, is contrasted with the first reading where Adam and Eve did give in. We'll never know precisely what their sin was, but it doesn't matter. Ultimately their sin was no different than ours, a decision not to trust God when he tells us to do or not to do something. Even though Adam and Eve gave in to sin, we can't be too condemning of them. We might not have done any better ourselves.

Temptation is always a matter of thinking we can be happier without God's direction or help. The grace to resist temptation is always available to us, but we don't always use it. All of us are tempted. Even Jesus himself was tempted. Did you notice how Jesus always answered the devil with a quote from scripture. It shows how knowing scripture can be a real help to resist temptation. Then again, the devil quoted scripture too, so we have to know it well.

We always begin the season of Lent with Jesus in the desert. I want to say a word or two about the desert. Jesus was sent there by the Holy Spirit right after his baptism. It was a time to reflect and pray, a time of transition from the workshop to his work of teaching and healing. We all need to go into the desert from time to time. Sometimes the Holy Spirit takes us there by denying to us for a time the joys and consolations that we would like our religion to bring us. Sometimes life itself takes us into a desert, with the loss of a loved one or a job or our health, or a feeling that we've lost our purpose. Our faith is really tested during such times. That's when we wonder whether God still loves us, whether God is still with us. Lent is a kind of little desert as we are encouraged to temporarily back away from a few of life's pleasures, pleasures that distract us from reflecting on the more serious side of life. Often I minister to people who are dying. It's not unusual for someone to say to me: "I never thought this would happen to me." I guess they never thought about what was ahead for all of us. Life could be over for any of us tomorrow. The important thing to know is that eternal life is ahead for us too if we remain faithful to our Lord and follow him. Jesus told us he would prepare a place for us in his Father's home and he will never reject anyone who comes to him. But we do have the freedom to turn away from him by not following the way he has shown us. Indeed, these are profound thoughts, but that's what Lent is for, to think and pray about these things.

2nd Sunday of Lent
February 17, 2008

INTRODUCTION – (Genesis 12: 1-4a, 2 Timothy 1: 8b-10, Matthew 17: 1-9) Sin is a reality of life. We heard about that last week with the story of Adam and Eve. Grace, too, is a reality of life. St. Paul tells us God wants all people to be saved, which implies he will give each person sufficient grace for salvation. God's ways are often hidden from us, but his saving work became visible and a part of the history of the world with his call to Abraham. Abraham came from Sumer, a settlement near modern day Kuwait. He and his family migrated to

Haran, a city in the northern part of Syria, near Turkey. Eventually he heard God's call to leave his kinfolk behind and move to the land of Canaan, modern day Israel. He left behind a prosperous commercial area to settle in a land that was still relatively primitive and undeveloped. Abraham made the long and difficult journey at the tender age of 75 along with his wife, Sarah, who was 10 years younger. God was telling them, not only to pack up and move to an unknown territory, but to start a family there as well! It was a pure act of faith on the part of Abraham to follow God's call and to believe in the blessings God kept promising him, promises we hear in today's first reading.

HOMILY – We sang in the psalm refrain "Lord let your mercy be on us as we place our trust in you." Trust, or faith, in God is one of the most basic elements of our relationship with him. Without trust, our relationship will go nowhere. In the stories in the Bible about Abraham we see a man who trusted God totally. Peter, James and John get a boost to their faith on Mount Tabor with Jesus when they experienced Jesus' transfiguration.

I am sure many people here have climbed a mountain or high hill and experienced the presence and grandeur of God, maybe not as dramatic as the three apostles did in the transfiguration, but God's presence could be felt none the less. One of the most memorable days I ever had was the day I climbed Mt. Sinai, a mountain in the southern portion of Sinai Peninsula where tradition has it that God gave Moses the Ten Commandments. It is part of a chain of rugged, reddish colored granite mountains that rise high into the air. Mt. Sinai itself is 7500 feet high. The view of the stark and arid mountains surrounding Mt. Sinai is spectacular.

If you've never climbed a real mountain, I'm sure you've climbed many mountains figuratively: mountains of ignorance to become educated, mountains of fear to discover new strength and courage, mountains of hurt and sickness to find healing, mountains of pride to discover we are not the center of the universe. In conquering such everyday heights, we discover the God who never leaves us. Peter, James and John on Mt. Tabor discovered the God that was hidden within Jesus who was always with them.

The Church continues to encourage us to discover God's invisible presence with each of us through its many ministries. This Sunday we make an appeal for several of the ministries that are vital to thousands of people within our own Archdiocese. These ministries are worthy of our support and in need of it. Such ministries are the Athenaeum and the education it offers to prospective priests, deacons and lay ministers; St. Rita's School for the Deaf, Catholic Social Services which helps with a great variety of social needs from adoption to care for the elderly, chaplains in hospitals and prisons and on college campuses and last but not least, retired priests. We are asking for your support today for all of these ministries which are grouped together under the name of the Catholic Ministries Appeal.

The name Catholic Ministries Appeal is now being used because the focus of the appeal has been totally directed only to these ministries not to any other programs or projects. Our goal is $15,000, the same as it was last year for the Archdiocesan Appeal. We made it last year. I'm sure we can do it again.

You will find an envelope in the pew which I ask you to fill out. You can make a pledge or an outright gift. If you make a gift through a check, please make it out to St. Boniface Church. Whether you are giving cash, a check or using your charge card, please drop the envelope in the collection or send it in the mail to St. Boniface. You can take it home and bring it next week if that's convenient.

Are you wondering how much to give in order to help us reach our goal? My suggestion would be to give about two and a half times what you give as a donation on an average Sunday. Thus if you give $20 a week (or $80 a month as some people choose to do), then donate $50 to this special appeal (that's 2 1/2 times $20). If you give $40 a week, than donate $100 (2 1/2 times 40). I think we'll make our goal that way. Some people cannot donate any more than they now are giving, so if you can do better than 2 1/2 times your Sunday donation that will help make up for those who cannot give so much. Just remember to make checks out to St. Boniface Church and whether you make a pledge, give cash, check or use a charge card, return the envelope to us.

3rd Sunday of Lent
February 24, 2008

HOMILY – (Exodus 17:3-7, Romans 5:1-2, 5-8, John 4:5-42) Samaria was located half way between Galilee and Jerusalem. It covered an area roughly the size of Butler and Hamilton County put together. The trip from Galilee to Jerusalem took about three days on foot if the journey went through Samaria, but because of the animosity between the Jews and the Samaritans, often travelers would go around Samaria, making their trip longer. Jesus and his disciples took the shorter route, and they were about half way through Samaria when the events in today's gospel took place. It was around noon and probably getting warm. Jesus sat down to rest. Most of the women in the vicinity would have been at the well early in the morning to get the water they needed for the day. Perhaps the woman in today's gospel came to draw water at noon in order to avoid nasty looks or comments from the other women who may have looked down their noses at her because of her current unmarried situation. For any number of reasons, Jesus could have easily slipped away when she arrived. In addition to her unconventional living arrangement, she was a woman and a Samaritan. Jews had nothing to do with Samaritans and men usually did not speak with women in public. Rabbis would not even talk with their own wives in public. But Jesus did not walk away. Rather he asked for a drink.

I was on vacation last week. The priest at the church which I attended on the weekend preached for 25 minutes. I could easily talk for 25 minutes on today's gospel, there are so many details that could be pointed out. But I won't do that to you. There are a couple of things that do deserve a special mention.

Water is a major theme of the gospel. Jesus asked for a drink then offered the woman living water. The term was deliberately ambiguous. Ordinary people, of course, didn't have running water in their homes. That's why they all had to come to a well nearby to draw water. The woman interpreted the term "living water" to mean a fountain or a spring. She had no idea that the living water Jesus was talking about was water that would lead to eternal life. Life, as we all know, depends on water. Recently in the news they have been talking about whether there was water on the planet Mars and if so how recently it existed there. The main issue, of course, is if water was there at one time, then life could have existed there too. There is no life without water.

Similarly, we Christians see our own beginning in the life of grace starting with the water, the water of baptism.

Another feature of today's gospel is to notice this woman gradually coming to know Jesus in a fuller and deeper way. She initially addresses Jesus as "sir," a polite title, then she recognizes him as a prophet, then she begins to believe he is the Christ, that is, the Messiah. In her excitement she forgot about the water she came to get (St. John tells us she left her water jar at the well) and she ran into town to tell everyone about him. The town itself concluded that he was even more than the Jewish Messiah, the savior of the Jews, but he was truly the savior of the world. [It is a journey parallel to the journey taken by those in the RCIA as they seek to know more and more about Jesus on their way to entering the Church at Easter.]

It might be worth noting that historically, after the resurrection of Jesus and the coming of the Holy Spirit on the Apostles at Pentecost, the Samaritans were very receptive to the preaching of the Apostles. Perhaps the events narrated in today's gospel paved the way for their conversion.

Everything in today's gospel started with a conversation between Jesus and the woman. And this is the point that impresses me the most. We'll never get to know the Lord if we don't take time to talk with him. He doesn't show up in radiant light or thunder and lightening. He comes in ordinary ways, in the guise of a friend or even an adversary, in the words from a book, especially The Book which we call by its Greek name, the Bible. He shows up in an assembly of believers and in such simple things as water, bread and wine. The important thing is to make time to listen, to respond, to have a conversation, to do more than just tell him what we want him to do for us. We never get to know anyone in life without spending time with them. If the Lord is important to us, we need to set time aside to spend with him too. Amen.

4th Sunday of Lent
March 2, 2008

INTRODUCTION – (1 Samuel 16: 1b,6-7,10-13a, Ephesians 5: 8-14, John 9: 1-41) Sight is a wonderful gift, but what we see with our mind and heart is even of greater value. God helps us to see clearly. We have examples of that inner vision in all of today's readings. Our first reading takes us back 1000 years before Christ when the prophet Samuel had to choose a king from among the sons of Jesse of Bethlehem. They all had the dignity and physical characteristics of potentially good leaders, but God knew who would make the best king. Paul tells us we have been enlightened by Christ and in the gospel we hear how a man born blind not only had his eyes opened by Christ but his heart, whereas those who claimed to be able to see were blinded by arrogance.

HOMILY – Two weeks ago, I appealed to all of our parishioners for their support of the Catholic Ministries Appeal. It is going well. We are about $2500 short of our $15,000 goal. I am most grateful to all who have responded. There has been one item that a few people have been confused about. In past years, at this time of the year, we have had the Archdiocesan Fund Drive. Some are wondering if another appeal is coming next. The answer is: No!

I wanted to make another appeal to you today, not for money, but for your involvement at Mass. You might have noticed that last week and this week we've been singing some hymns you might not have heard for years, such as All the Earth Proclaim the Lord; Yes, I Shall Arise; My Soul is Longing for Your Peace. Next week you will hear them again. I have asked Don to schedule these pieces in testimony to their composer: Fr. Lucien Deiss. Fr. Deiss died about five months ago and he was a pioneer in composing liturgical music 45 years ago as the language of the Mass was going from Latin to English. He was also a scholar in Sacred Scripture and Patristics (that is the study of the early Fathers of the Church). I had the opportunity to attend a workshop by him when I was first ordained and I was deeply impressed. Much of his music is no longer in use today (except for Keep in Mind) but I thought his passing should not go unnoticed.

I thought I would take this occasion as we remember him, to stress the importance of music at Mass. I've told you my story about when I was a child, whenever we had singing practice, the good sisters in school encouraged me to listen. They said that way I would learn to sing if I listened to the others. It wasn't until I was 20 or 21 that our choir director in the seminary called me aside after chant practice and offered to give me individual lessons in singing. I think it helped. The point I'm trying to make is that if you think you can't sing, you'll never learn how if you don't try. Sometimes people say to me I don't know that hymn we had today. But if a person doesn't try to sing it they'll never know it. I don't know if people have ever noticed but the hymns we choose try to correspond to the liturgical season and the theme of the readings. Hopefully, if a hymn is unfamiliar, over the course of time we will become more comfortable with it. We'll never learn any new ones any other way. I know that musical tastes vary. Some people like the more traditional ones and others like the more modern ones, some people like the slow, prayerful ones and some like those with a fast, lively beat. Don tries to vary them, I know. The important thing is that they represent quality music. But sometimes good music is not always appreciated right away. While I was on vacation, I watched a movie on the life of Cole Porter. There was a comment he made in the movie that struck me. He said "I often get paid much less for a really good piece of music than I get paid for that that's not very good." As with many other things in life, popularity does not represent quality and vice-versa. And the music we use should be good quality.

When everyone sings, the prayer is uplifting and energizing. Singing gets a person more involved and engaged in the Mass. And the time seems to go by quickly. I noticed when I can't sing (like if I have a sore throat), the time goes much more slowly. Maybe this is what St. Augustine meant when he said: "he who sings, prays twice." We put more of ourselves is into the prayer when we sing. I have two suggestions: if people would more up further in church, they could support one another with their singing and this would give more a sense of community. The other suggestion is to open your hymn book to the hymn and if you can't sing it or don't feel comfortable even trying, just read the words that are being sung, for they are a prayer. That's all I'll say. The more involved you are in the Mass, the more a blessing it will be for you. Amen.

5th Sunday of Lent
March 9, 2008

HOMILY – (Ezekiel 37: 12-14, Romans 8: 8-11, John 11: 1-45) Bertrand Russell said: success is getting what you want; happiness is wanting what you get. I don't think many of us wanted all this snow, but what Bertrand Russell said implies that we do our best to adjust to the ups and downs of life. Thank God we have our faith to help us along the way and to give us hope.

The greatest hope we have is that life will never end.

Today's gospels is one of my very favorite ones, because it was while I was visiting the tomb of Lazarus in Bethany that I had an overwhelming experience of the divine presence of Jesus.

Jesus said to Martha: "I am the resurrection and the life; whoever believes in me, even if he dies, will live, and everyone who lives and believes in me will never die." Who could make such a statement: "everyone who lives and believes in me will never die?" They would either have to be someone so unique and special, the likes of which this world has never known, or they would have to be someone severely delusional. From everything else we know about Jesus, he was totally sane and in touch with reality. More than that he was someone with special wisdom and special powers. He did not just ask for Martha's faith, "do you believe this?" but he did more, he showed he had power even over death itself. Who else has the power to make the tombs empty? The Lord asks us today as he asked Martha: "Do you believe this?" "Do you believe that everyone who lives and believes in me will never die?" What a comfort this is when we lose a loved one whom we know has lived and died in God's grace.

But Jesus' words are not limited to the experience of death. We all experience many losses in life, little deaths, things that we have to grieve for. It could be our health, our job, our security or the loss of something that meant a lot to us. We have to trust somehow that even in these sufferings God can bring life out of death. This is what is meant by the Easter mystery, or the Paschal mystery that we are preparing to celebrate. As St. Paul tells us: "We know that all things work for good for those who love God." Rom 8,28.

This is the hope that I live by and that gives new life to all of us. Amen.

Passion Sunday
March 16, 2008

HOMILY – (Matthew 21: 1-11, Philippians 2: 6-11, Matthew 26:14 – 27:66) Without the resurrection, Jesus' life and ministry would have been a total disaster. Sure he taught profound truths, he healed the sick, he drove out demons, but all his good work would have come to a frustrating and disappointing end. Nothing would have come of all that he did. It's not likely his followers who all deserted him, except for John and a few women, would have ever mentioned his name again except among themselves. We would probably never have heard of him or of the message of love that he preached. He died an accused criminal by one of the most painful forms of death ever invented by human beings. He was a victim of hatred, power, jealousy, and greed.

In a lesser way, at times other people's lives seem to end in failure. A good person may die and be quickly forgotten. Or it may happen that no matter how hard a person tries, no matter how much good they do, a tragedy occurs, one's efforts seem to go unrewarded, something happens that a person's reputation is destroyed, a lifetime relationship falls apart and the good things a person has done is buried with them. Shakespeare's words about Julius Caesar have described the lives of so much of suffering humanity: "the evil that men do lives after them, the good is oft interred with their bones."

Shakespeare's words would have been true of Jesus too, regarding the few who knew him, if there had not been a resurrection. But the story of Jesus is not over; our stories are never over either. This week we will follow the journey of Jesus through disaster and death to resurrection and new life. To help us as we make that journey we are given his body and blood as our food and drink to nourish us and give us life – his risen life. If we follow him with faith our stories of love and good works can be as his story was, a story of love poured out that cannot be overcome by failure, a story of life that is not overcome by death. Amen.

Holy Thursday
March 20, 2008

HOMILY – (Exodus 12:1-8, 11-14, 1 Corinthians 11:23-26, John 13:1-15) When Jews gather for the Passover, which is described in the first reading, the youngest child asks: "why is this night different from all other nights?" The head of the family answered the question by describing how God saved his people from slavery and brought them to the Promised Land. The more I thought about tonight and how I would answer the question "why is this night different from all other nights" the more ideas came to mind. Don't worry, I'm not going to try to put all that could be said into my homily tonight. As a matter of fact, we could spend the rest of our lives reflecting on the central elements of our faith that we celebrate tonight and still not exhaust all the meaning they contain.

So I want to reflect on the virtue of faith as it is demanded by the Eucharist, and the virtue of love as it is demonstrated in the washing of feet. I think the Eucharist is the greatest test of our faith for Catholics today. It is a test I believe the statistics on Mass attendance show is too much for many Catholics to cope with. It challenges our minds to accept that the Son of God, who took on human flesh, could just as easily take on the form of bread and wine and become our food and drink. In tonight's gospel Peter could not imagine that their master and Lord would stoop to wash their feet. Jesus said "you don't understand it now, but you will understand it later." Peter's response was "you'll never wash my feet." Jesus said "unless I wash you, you will have no inheritance with me." In other words Jesus said to Peter: you just have to believe me that what I am doing for you will keep us united throughout eternity (what else could Jesus have meant by his inheritance). These words are amazingly similar to what Jesus said earlier in John's gospel about the Eucharist: "unless you eat the flesh of the son of man and drink his blood you do not have life within you." Peter had to simply take Jesus on his word even if what Jesus was doing didn't make sense to him. In the Eucharist we have to simply take Jesus on his word, "this is my body," even if what Jesus says doesn't make sense to us.

Scientists tell us today there are certain foods that nourish us and certain foods that are of little value or that can even be harmful to us. The foods that truly nourish us do so, not because they look or taste wonderful, but because of certain invisible nutrients in the food. So when Jesus said, "the bread that I will give is my flesh for the life of the world," if we believe him to be trustworthy, then we will trust that there is something in this food that will give us eternal life – we don't know how. Paul tells us that tonight in the second reading which is the oldest written account of the Eucharist. As I said at the beginning, I could contemplate this for the rest of my life and still probably would not understand. But as Jesus said: "you will understand later."

The second main idea this evening's liturgy focuses on is love and service. Have you ever wondered why we have the gospel of the washing of the feet tonight and not focus entirely on the Eucharist? I think the reason is that the Church wants us to know that love and service is as important as the Eucharist, for without love, as Paul said: "I am nothing." Since actions speak louder than words, Jesus gave us an example in action to help us remember how important it is. The washing of feet was the task of a servant for who would enjoy washing feet when people had to walk dusty, dirty roads where animals as well as humans walked? But Jesus' act of humility in washing the apostles' feet was only a preview of his great act of humility in giving his life for us on the cross. Lest we forget this act of love and service, he asked us to "do it in remembrance of me." Notice in the reading from Paul Jesus says this twice because it's so important – so important that we not forget.

"Why is this night different from all other nights?" When this question was answered at the Passover supper with the description of God saving his people, the answer helped the youngest child (and everyone else at the dinner) to gain a sense of their identity as God's people. When we gather here tonight we are given, through the liturgy, a sense of our identity as God's people, followers of Jesus Christ who gather here in faith to celebrate his memory, to receive him as our food and drink and to love one another.

Good Friday
March 25, 2005

HOMILY – (Isaiah 52:13–53:12, Hebrews 4:14-16; 5:7-9, John 18:1–19:42) He was born and grew up in an obscure village, the child of ordinary people. He worked as a carpenter and an itinerant preacher. He never wrote a book, never held an office, never had a wife or children, nor owned a house. He never traveled two hundred miles from the place where he was born. When he was only thirty-three his enemies had him nailed to a cross. His executioners gambled for his clothing. He was laid in a borrowed grave. After nineteen centuries he is the central figure of the human race. All the kings that ever reigned, all the armies that ever marched have not affected the human race as much as that one solitary life.

So many times I am asked why Christ died as he did? For one thing, everything would be different. I'm sure when many of us have read history we've asked ourselves what would things be like if a certain event hadn't happened. What if Columbus had not been so determined to sail to the West Indies? Or what if the British had crushed the revolution of their thirteen colonies here in the new world in the late 1700's? Or what if the South had won the Civil War in 1864? Or what if Mr. and Mrs. Edison had decided to stop having children after their sixth one? Thomas Alva Edison, who was their seventh child, would not have been born. It's interesting to speculate how our lives would have been different if one person or one event had not been. But what about Jesus? What if he hadn't died as he did?

Maybe being divine he would have been taken up directly into heaven without having to die. If, like Elijah, he was carried to heaven in a fiery chariot, some obscure Jewish history book might have mentioned him, but would that gain him a great following? Or, since Jesus was also human like us in every way except sin, he may have died a natural death, which would have resulted in his soon being forgotten after all his followers died. Think about it. Do you suppose, in either case, his followers would have risked their lives to go out preaching about him or would anyone have taken the time to write down what he said or did? Would any of us have even heard about him?

Perhaps we would still be worshipping Jupiter and Mars and Venus, or sacrificing our children to Baal or Moloch. In pagan mythology, humans were not loved by the gods. Humans were only useful to the gods for the sacrifices and worship they offered. Would we have ever heard the message of God's love and mercy? Or perhaps somewhere along the line, our ancestors might have recognized the superiority of the Jewish faith over paganism and we would all be observing Jewish traditions, abstaining from pork and making sure our infant boys were circumcised. Or maybe we all would have no spiritual anchor, wondering what life is all about, wondering if there is any kind of life after we die, wondering how God or the gods want us to serve him or her or them?

I strongly suspect that if Jesus did not die as he did and rise again, at least a billion people in today's world would be thinking, praying, acting, living differently than they are now, and with many people living life differently, everyone else would be affected.

When I am asked why did Jesus have to die as he did, one answer that can be given is that we probably would never have known about him if he hadn't. That's far from a complete answer to the question, though. Theologians have struggled with this question for centuries and they have come up with many different answers. So I would like to reflect on just a couple of other ways to look at the passion of Jesus.

We can't just look as his death in isolation from the rest of his life. His whole life was dedicated to teaching God's ways and assuring us of God's love. He came to tell us God has wonderful plans for us if we believe in him and follow him. His death was the culmination of a life of love. His teachings threatened the powerful people of his day. They were so threatened by him that they felt they had to kill him. However, Jesus loved his Father enough to stay with the job he had been given, to preach the truth. And he loved the people enough to keep teaching them, no matter what the consequences might be. He could have easily given up preaching, he could have gone into hiding, he could have gotten twelve legions of angels to give him security. But if he had done anything other than be faithful to his mission, he would have betrayed the unfailing and never-ending love he proclaimed.

We could talk for hours, and still not exhaust the meaning and significance of Jesus' passion. That's why we commemorate it every week, every day even! By his death he taught us how to be patient in suffering, and to hope in the face of defeat. He taught us that goodness can overcome evil and sin, and that death does not have the last word. And in his death and resurrection he gave us a new way to pray. The night before he died he gave us the greatest prayer there is – the Eucharist. It is a prayer that unites us with him in his saving death and resurrection, and it is a prayer that shows us the perfection of faithfulness and love and gives us the help to model our lives on it.

We've all bought things that we have to assemble ourselves. Someone manufactured the item, and packed it in a box and then left it to us to put together. Jesus has done everything possible to make eternal life available to us. But we have to do the job of incorporating Jesus' saving work into our own lives. We can't leave it in the box and expect it to work. We have to live it each day. Today we honor Jesus' sacrifice and love. We pray we will do what we need to do to make it a part of our lives.

Easter
March 23, 2008

HOMILY – (Acts 10: 34a, 37-43, Colossians 3: 1-4, John 20: 1-9) Children say the darndest things. When a family with a small child showed up at church on Easter Sunday, the little child wondered why all the decorations and flowers. His mother explained that we were celebrating Jesus' resurrection after he died on the cross. The child exclaimed "Jesus died!? Jesus died!? When did that happen? Why didn't you tell me?" (They must have missed Mass on Palm Sunday).

At an Easter Sunday Mass in church, a mother heard her five-year-old daughter singing joyfully "lasagna in the highest!"

A father told about his little four-year-old's excitement over what the Easter bunny would bring on Easter. The father asked if his son knew what Easter was really about. The very bright little boy answered: "Jesus died on the cross, so we can live with him in heaven some day." Then he added: "But I don't want to die." The father said, everyone has to die sometime, but we hope it will not be for a long time." The boy replied: "okay, but if there's no TV in heaven, I'm leaving."

Last year at this time James Cameron, director of the movie Titanic, produced a program for the Discovery

Channel entitled The Lost Tomb of Jesus. It seems that in 1980 there were several first century caskets or bone boxes found in a tomb outside of Jerusalem and one of them had the inscription on it: Jesus son of Joseph. The dead person's bones were still in the casket. From other bits of information connected with this particular casket, Mr. Cameron concluded that he had discovered Jesus' body and he modestly proclaimed this was the "greatest archaeological find of all time." Like the famous ship in his movie Titanic, it wasn't long before Mr. Cameron's boast about the "greatest archaeological find of all time" ran into an iceberg and began to sink. Expert archaeologists from around the world who had examined the casket and the tomb cast strong doubt on the so-called discovery of Jesus' dead body and the sensation created by the program began to fade.

All through the centuries people have tried to explain away the resurrection of Jesus, beginning with the Roman soldiers who were sent to guard the tomb and who claimed they fell asleep while they were on guard and the apostles came and stole Jesus' body. Any one can easily see the contradiction in this. The resurrection of Jesus is a matter of faith, for no one witnessed it, except perhaps the Roman guards who were paid to tell a different story.

My faith in the resurrection has been a great source of strength and comfort for me. However, I do not believe simply because that faith brings me comfort. My faith rests on two pieces of solid evidence: first, an empty tomb over which Constantine built the Church of the Holy Sepulcher in 335 A.D. and which has been and still is venerated as the tomb of Jesus right from the beginning. And secondly, the testimony of Jesus' followers who had nothing to gain from proclaiming Jesus' resurrection except their own martyrdom. They would never have had the courage to preach about Jesus and the world would never have heard of him if Jesus hadn't risen and appeared to them many times and if the Holy Spirit hadn't come to them.

Our belief too, as St. Paul tells us, is not only that Jesus rose from the dead to live in eternal glory, but it is a glory we hope to share with him some day. No matter how powerful and final is the force of death, because of Jesus' resurrection, we Christians believe that life has the final word – not death and it is life eternal. This is why St. Paul tells us to "think of what is above, not what is on earth." Of course we have to provide for our everyday needs and, in love, provide for the needs of our brothers and sisters in this world, but we have to avoid living only for this world. Our Mass each week helps to stay focused on what Jesus did for us and what is ahead for us if we remain faithful to him.

Please make the Mass something more than a once or twice a year event. So much happens in our busy lives that we need to be guided weekly, if not more often, with the word of God and nourished with the body and blood of Christ who died and rose for us. Amen.

Second Sunday of Easter
April 3, 2005

HOMILY – (Acts 2:42-47, 1 Peter 1:3-9, John 20:19-31) Jesus didn't rise just for himself or just to show off that he could overcome the power of death. St. Paul tells us Jesus "was handed over for our transgressions and was raised for our justification." (Rom 4, 25) Or as we say in one of the acclamations after the Consecration: "Dying you destroyed our death, rising your restored our life…" We are used to thinking that after we die, our spirit moves on to wherever it's going: heaven, hell or purgatory and we'll be like angels from then on. Indeed our spirit does move on, but that's not the end of the story. We are not angels and never will be. Our spirit without our body is incomplete. Part of being human is to have a body, and Christ showed us in his resurrection what his plan is for all of us who believe in him and are faithful to him. Again we quote Paul: In the resurrection of the dead, our body "is sown corruptible; it is raised incorruptible. It is sown dishonorable; it is raised glorious. It is sown weak; it is raised powerful. It is sown a natural body; it is raised a spiritual body." (1 Cor 15, 42-44) We proclaim this doctrine every Sunday, "We look for the resurrection of the dead, and the life of the world to come."

In the midst of our celebration of the resurrection, the news has been preoccupied with death, the death of our Holy Father and the death of Terry Shiavo. I do not wish to slight the Holy Father, but I think I should give some teaching about medical moral issues connected with Terry Shiavo's death. I didn't prepare to say anything about the Holy Father this week because I didn't know when he would die.

When I was in the seminary, we learned in medical moral ethics that when a person is dying it is not necessary to use extraordinary measures to keep them alive. After all, death is the natural end to life in this world. A person could, of course, use whatever extraordinary measures were available to them, but they didn't have to. I think the death of the Holy Father illustrates this. Probably he could have gone to the hospital and they could have hooked up all kinds of machines on him to keep him alive for another few days or weeks or months, but he chose to stay at the Vatican and let nature take its course. Many times I have used this principal (that a person can, but does not have to use extraordinary measures to prolong life) in counseling a family whose loved one was near death and who was being kept alive in a purely artificial way. Often times this principal applied to people dying of cancer, when extraordinary measures would simply prolong their suffering.

When we are dealing with a person who is in what is called a vegetative state, it becomes a little more difficult to know where to draw the line and that principle becomes more controversial. The general practice has been that if a person was in a permanent vegetative state, all life support could be, but not necessarily had to be, terminated. With Terry Shiavo, there was some controversy about whether she was in a permanent vegetative state. This is one of the problems with that diagnosis.

A year ago, the Holy Father addressed physicians, scientists and ethicists from over forty countries. He began by stating that medical science is still unable to predict with certainty who among patients in this condition will recover and who will not. He considers the word "vegetative" as a poor choice of words as a human being, even if seriously ill or disabled in the exercise of his highest functions, is and always will be a human being, and he will never become a "vegetable" or an "animal."

He went on to say that the sick person in a vegetative state ...still has the right to basic health care (nutrition, hydration, cleanliness, warmth, etc.). He especially emphasized that the administration of water and food, even when provided by artificial means, always represents a natural means of preserving life, not a medical act. Its use should be considered, in principle, ordinary and proportionate, and as such morally obligatory. His words apply clearly to Terry Shiavo:

"Death by starvation or dehydration is, in fact, the only possible outcome as a result of their withdrawal. In this sense it ends up becoming, if done knowingly and willingly, true and proper euthanasia by omission." The Holy Father seems to admit to an exception to this principle when administering water or nutrition does not benefit the patient, but only serves to increase their suffering.

We get into a very dangerous area when we start using "quality of life" judgments about who should be allowed to live and who shouldn't. Who is going to draw that line?

Just a week ago my aunt died. She was 95 and had suffered with Alzheimer's for many years. She did not have a feeding tube, but was being fed intravenously. I do not know whether the Holy Father's remarks include such things as intravenous feeding. That's one of the questions I have about his address. As the family wrestled with taking her off intravenous feeding, they felt as if they would be killing her if they did, so they didn't. I'm sure their decision gave them some peace.

I'm not sure if all possible questions about this issue have been answered, but in view of what happened this past week, and in view of the fact that many of our families have to face these kind of issues from time to time, I felt something should be said to clarify the Church's stand on this. If there is an error to be made, the Church always prefers to err on the side of life.

Third Sunday of Easter
April 6, 2008

INTRODUCTION – (Acts 2: 14, 22-33, 1 Peter 1: 17-21, Luke 24: 13-35) In our first reading we hear

Peter's first sermon which was on Pentecost Sunday. Just a few weeks prior to this speech he denied he even knew Jesus. Now he speaks out boldly about Jesus. I want to call your attention to one little detail. We are told he stood up "with the Eleven." It's one of many places in the gospels that the position of Peter is shown as primary among the rest of the apostles. This coming week our Holy Father, the successor of St. Peter, will make a short visit to our country.

HOMILY – Today's gospel is a story of discouragement and hope. We all experience discouragements and disappointment at times throughout our lives. We even get discouraged with God. St. Luke tells us a story today about how two people met with discouragement after seeing how Jesus had been put to death. They had hoped he would drive the Romans out of Israel and restore freedom and self-government to Israel. When Jesus died their hopes were shattered and they walked away. How often we want to walk away from God when he doesn't do the things we want him to.

Briefly, let us recall the events in today's gospel. Jesus joined his two disciples and entered into conversation with them. They didn't recognize him. He explained to them from the Scriptures that it was necessary for the Messiah to suffer as he did. As evening approached they invited him to stay with them. He did, and broke bread with them and then they recognized him. They returned to Jerusalem to the apostles and believers.

Even when we turn our back on God, he doesn't turn his back on us. St. Luke wants us to know that even in our discouragement and disappointment we are not alone. We may not recognize God's presence as we go. But it's there. Most of us remember the poem that was very popular a few years ago: footprints in the sand. He promised us: "I will be with you always."

St. Luke is telling us also that in hard times, the Scriptures can throw new light on the difficulties we are having. Jesus helped his two disciples to understand the Scriptures better, renewing their hope. As they said "Were not our hearts burning within us as he spoke to us on the way and opened the Scriptures to us." I can't count how many times that has happened to me that when I felt discouraged, God's word lifted my spirits. God's word is always a word that gives hope.

As the story goes on, the disciples invited Jesus to stay with them longer. What was happening there? Did they, for a moment, forget about their own sadness to think about the safety of this stranger? Travel in those days was dangerous, especially to travel by oneself. Or was Jesus beginning to get through to them and they didn't want their time with him to come to an end? For whatever reason they asked him to stay longer.

Before they knew it, Jesus was breaking bread with them and suddenly they recognized Jesus and they knew he was alive. Luke doesn't really tell us this was a Eucharist, but notice the words Luke uses to describe what Jesus did: Jesus took the bread, said the blessing, broke it and gave it to them. These are the same gestures St. Luke used to describe what Jesus did at the Last Supper. Furthermore, whenever St. Luke always refers to the Eucharist in the Acts of the Apostles, (the other book he wrote) he call it the Breaking of the Bread. If it wasn't a Eucharist Jesus did with the two disciples, St. Luke certainly has this in mind when he tells us this is when the disciples recognized who they had been talking to all this time.

There is one last piece to this story, the two disciples returned to community of believers. They had given up their hope in Jesus as the savior of God's people and they walked away from the community of those still gathered in Jerusalem who believed in him. Their encounter with Christ on the road, in the Scriptures, in the hospitality they offered him, in the breaking of bread restored all their hope and joy. And they came back to the Church, the community of believers they had left. It is there they would continue to remain united with Christ.

When disappointment fills our lives with sadness and darkness, we can let it consume us or we can let God help us find light and healing, for God is our only hope.

Fourth Sunday of Easter
April 13, 2008

HOMILY – (Acts 2: 14a, 36-41, 1 Peter 2: 20b-25, John 10: 1-10) Modern shepherds often control their sheep with dogs, horses, pick-up trucks or other advanced technological methods. Shepherds in the ancient world didn't have such methods and they guarded and guided their sheep themselves. Shepherds make their living caring for sheep and, since sheep require full time care, they were together almost constantly with their sheep. Old time shepherds gave each lamb its own name just as we give names to our pets. Like our pets recognize our voice and come running when we call them, unless they're cats, which are very independent, so also the sheep came running when their shepherd called.

Even though we do not see real sheep and shepherds very often, still the image of the good shepherd is one of the most comforting images in the Scriptures. The best remembered and loved psalm of all 150 psalms is Psalm 23: "The Lord is my shepherd." It symbolizes God's protection and care and guidance. But there are two sides to that coin. If he is to be our shepherd and protector, he expects that we will follow him. We will hear his voice.

A second image Jesus used in today's gospel is that he is the gate of the sheepfold. Whoever goes in and out through him will be safe and find pasture. Gates serve the same function as doors. Think of how important doors are. They let us in our homes where we find safety and family. They let us go out so we can meet friends or make a living or buy things we need or do something fun. They close out people who shouldn't be there. Jesus is telling us as doors and gates are important so is he. When he is part of our comings and goings, when we make him central in our lives, when we ask his blessing on all our activities, our life will be secure and our happiness will be ensured.

Does this mean nothing bad will ever happen if we follow Christ? If it were true that if we do everything God wants, God would do everything we want, church would be packed every week. I know there are rewards in this life when we stay faithful to him. I have certainly tried to stay on God's good side and God has been very good to me, but as we all know bad things do happen to good people. Even many of Jesus' good friends suffered, some were even tortured and put to death as Jesus was. But it's not just to protect us in this world that Jesus came. The last verse in today's gospel is one of my favorites. Jesus said "I came so that they might have life and have it more abundantly." Or as it's sometimes translated: "I came so that they might have life and have it to the full." When people ask why Jesus doesn't keep bad things from happening to those who are faithful to him, perhaps one answer could be that life in this world is not where the abundant life really is. Even if we have looks, popularity, health, wealth, youth, wisdom and everything else our hearts desire, we don't "have it all."

We'll always feel some emptiness in our hearts, we'll never be totally satisfied, because our hearts were made for perfect union with God, and we won't know what that's like until we get to heaven. Our faith is that's where Christ our shepherd wants to lead us and that's why he came to us.

Fifth Sunday of Easter
April 20, 2008

INTRODUCTION – (Acts 6: 1-7, 1 Peter 2: 4-9, John 14: 1-12) Three weeks ago we heard St. Luke tell us in the Acts of the Apostles how the first Christians got along so beautifully. They devoted themselves to prayer and instruction from the Apostles and generously shared their material possessions so that no one was in need among them. As the community grew, so did the problems. The first Christians were probably conservative Jews from around Jerusalem who spoke Hebrew or Aramaic. They were culturally and traditionally different from converted Jews who lived in other parts of the Roman Empire and who spoke the common language of the day, Greek. They are referred to in today's first reading as the Hellenists. Besides this cultural difference, there were economic issues. Widows in those days were entirely dependent on the community for their basic needs. The Hellenists, those who spoke Greek, complained that their widows were being discriminated against when food was being given out at Christian gatherings. The Apostles felt their role was not to give out food but to stay focused on prayer and preaching so they solved the problem by creating a new office in the Church, the diaconate.

HOMILY – Our gospel reading puts us at the Last

Supper with Jesus and the Apostles. Jesus knew that the Apostles' world would soon be turned upside down. In spite of repeated warnings, the Apostles were not ready for what was going to take place once they left the Supper room. So he gave them one last word of wisdom: "don't be troubled, don't be afraid, just trust me." What an order! In spite of Jesus' words not to be troubled, they were devastated after he was arrested and put to death. If Jesus' words at that time did not give much comfort to the Apostles, they have been giving comfort in times of suffering to all the rest of us for the past 2000 years. They are reflected in a very popular hymn: "Be not afraid."

Jesus describes to them why they should not be troubled or afraid: because there would be a better life ahead for them and he was going away to prepare a place for them so they could be with him forever. He told them there were many "dwelling places" in his Father's house. Sometimes the word "dwelling places" is translated "mansions." We have to carefully understand just what Jesus is saying here. Too often we interpret his words in a materialistic way, thinking of multi-million dollar homes we will have in heaven as a reward for being good. Some people may even picture a Mercedes in the garage, a pool in the back yard, a well-stocked wine cellar in the basement and 70 virgins waiting to meet them. This kind of a vision reduced happiness to sheer materialism and that is not what happiness with God will be all about. The Greek word translated as "dwelling place" does not mean "mansion." The word puts emphasis, not so much on a building or structure, as on the act of staying or dwelling. Reading further on in John's gospel we learn that the "Father's house" where Jesus is going and where there are many "dwelling places" is really to be understood as the experience of communion with God and with Jesus and being able to share in God's glory. This will be a source of joy that is greater than anything we can know in this world. This may be a disheartening thought for those who are looking for material rewards or untold physical pleasures.

St. Paul tells us "What no one ever saw or heard, what no one ever thought could happen, is the very thing God prepared for those who love him." (Translation: Good News Bible – 1 Cor 2,9) What's ahead for us is beyond our understanding. True, Jesus did use images we could understand to give us a hint of what heaven would be like. Heaven is like a hidden treasure, a pearl of great worth, a wedding banquet a king has for his son, a place without sadness or suffering or death. His examples can be very comforting to think about and can motivate us to live a holy life. What is more important to think about, though, is not what we'll find when we enter into the next life as the way that leads there. It's of major importance because if we don't go the right way, we won't end up in the right place. Our culture today tells us it doesn't matter what way we follow, we'll all end up in the same place. That's not what Jesus tells us. Jesus tells us today "I am the way, the truth and the life. No one comes to the Father except through me." He is not only the way, but also the truth. Contrary to founders of certain different religions who have told their followers they have found the truth, Jesus goes further and tells us he is the truth! It is in him, in Jesus, we will see the glory of God as he tells Philip today. When Philip asked to be able to see the Father, Philip was thinking as we often do, that somehow God is hiding somewhere and if he would only show himself to us we would be happy. We don't realize how much he wants us to see him and know him, to share his life and to know his joy. God is not made of material things. He can't come out of hiding because he is not hiding from us. He is all around us, but we can only know him through a faith that fills our minds and hearts, and Jesus has pointed that way of faith out to us.

While I was praying the other day, the image of Jesus as a compass came to mind. A compass always points north. I don't understand exactly how magnetism works, but I know if I follow the way it points, it will not mislead me. I don't understand God perfectly either, because God is infinite and the infinite is too great for my finite mind. But I trust in Jesus, and I know that if I follow the way he points, he will not mislead me. He is the way, the truth and the life.

Sixth Sunday of Easter
April 27, 2008

INTRODUCTION – (Acts 8: 5-8, 14-17, 1 Peter 3: 15-18, John 14: 15-21) Last week, in our first reading from the Acts of the Apostles, we heard about the institution of the diaconate, a word that comes from the Greek which means "service." Seven men were chosen by the community to care for the needs of the poor. In a short time, the first deacons did more than simply care for the poor. We have all heard of St. Stephen who became such a convincing preacher that his enemies killed him. He was the first martyr, a word that comes from the Greek that means witness. Today we hear about another of the original deacons, Philip. He too became a powerful healer and preacher and baptized many people into the faith of Christ. Baptizing continues to be part of the ministry of a deacon.

HOMILY – In today's gospel Jesus is talking with his Apostles at the Last Supper. He was trying to prepare them, as best he could, for the shock and trauma they would go through when he would be arrested and crucified. He had just told them, as we heard last Sunday, that he was going to go to get a place ready for them in his Father's home, then he would come to take them with him so they would be with him always. In today's gospel he tells them that, although he is leaving them for a time, he would not abandon them. First of all, he would give them another Advocate. (The Greek word here for Advocate is παράκλητος which is hard to translate). Often it is left untranslated and is put into English as paraclete. When translators try to translate it, they use words like "Advocate," "Comforter," "Intercessor," "Helper," "Mediator." It means, basically, someone who will support you, stand up for you, or stand by your side to help you. Of course, Jesus was referring to the Holy Spirit. Jesus was not planning on leaving them with a substitute for himself for he said to them: "I will not leave you orphans. I will come to you. In a little while the world will no longer see me, but you will see me…" In other words, the Holy Spirit would be with them in addition to Jesus, but Jesus would be with them in a new way, a way they would know only through the help of the Spirit.

There are so many themes packed into today's readings, and I can only touch on a few of these ideas. One of the important themes is love. It is out of love that Jesus gives us the Holy Spirit. From the beginning he has loved us and he asks only for our love in return. In our gospel today he gives us a criterion to keep us from thinking love is just a matter of having warm, fuzzy feelings toward him. The test of true love for Jesus is to do his will, just as he has always done the will of the Father. "If you love me, you will keep my commandments." He says it twice in today's short gospel.

In other words, love is measured more by what we do than by what we feel! I have found that to be such a hard message to get across to people. The attitude so many people have is: if they don't feel it, they don't think it is. It's not that feelings are bad. Having warm, loving feelings toward God or toward others is wonderful. But love has to go beyond just feelings or it's just superficial. Anyone who's married knows that!

Jesus describes the work of the Holy Spirit in numerous ways. Here he mentions two things about the Spirit: he tells us the Spirit will be with us always and he calls the Spirit the Spirit of Truth. I want to end with a little story I read recently. The partners at a huge New York law firm were discussing their most lucrative – and controversial – client: a gigantic chemical company. The managing partner summed up the situation: "Their billings are in excess of $100 million a year, and they pay like clockwork. But for that, can we justify defending them against polluting rivers and lakes, unlawful toxic dump sites and emitting poisonous gasses into the atmosphere?" Everyone on the board was silent until the senior partner spoke up. "You're right, entirely right. We should raise our fees."

Too often, life is like that. We use all kinds of defense mechanisms, rationalizations, justifications, denials, projections, etc. to avoid dealing with the truth. Jesus called the Paraclete the Spirit of Truth. Facing the truth without regard for profit, power, comfort, convention or popularity takes courage and help from the Holy Spirit. May the Spirit of Truth Christ gives us guide us to recognize the wisdom in his commands to us and to know his loving presence with us as we come to the Eucharist today. He is with us always; we have his word on that.

Seventh Sunday of Easter
May 16, 1999

HOMILY – (Acts 1:12-14, 1 Pet 4:13-16, John 17:1-11a) Jesus was asked one time what is the most important commandment in the law. We know how he answered. He not only gave us the most important commandment but the second most important commandment as well, two commands that perfectly compliment each other: to love God with our whole heart and soul and mind and strength and to love our neighbor as ourselves. Jesus gave us the answer not only by his words but also by the way he lived.

I would like to reflect today on how Jesus showed love for his Father. His perfect obedience was one way he showed his love. Another way he showed it was by spending time with his Father in prayer. That is what is especially want to focus on today. The topic of prayer was inspired by today's gospel which is part of Jesus prayer at the Last Supper. We have little or no information about what his life was like before he began his public ministry. The little information we do have shows us that Joseph and Mary were faithful in their Jewish observances. Thus Jesus would have been brought up in that tradition, going to synagogue on the Sabbath and going to the Temple in Jerusalem annually for Passover. St. Luke tells us that when Jesus was beginning his ministry he went to Nazareth and went to the synagogue on the Sabbath "according to his custom." Synagogue services would have been very similar to the first part of our Mass. There would be common prayer and readings from the Law and the prophets and with a commentary after each reading. St. Luke points out in his gospel that Jesus was praying as John the Baptist baptized him. Immediately after that, recall how Jesus went into the desert for 40 days to fast and pray. His encounter with the devil there showed he knew the scriptures well and he could quote them easily. Frequently it is mentioned that during his public ministry Jesus was at the Temple participating in liturgical celebrations there. The gospels tell us about Jesus getting up early in the morning to pray or staying up all night in prayer. He would spend time in prayer before important decisions or important events. One time after seeing Jesus praying, the disciples asked him to teach them to pray and of course we are all familiar with the prayer he taught them. In addition to the Our Father, Jesus taught a lot about prayer. For example the parable of a man who had a friend visit him at night and he went to his neighbor to borrow some food, and he kept on knocking until he got what he needed. That's the way Jesus said we should pray. Even when he wasn't teaching about prayer, his teachings reflect the deep relationship Jesus had with his Father. There is no doubt about it, prayer played a major role in Jesus life. The Last Supper of course was more than an ordinary supper. It was the Passover which Jesus was celebrating with his disciples, which was a religious celebration.

His prayer (in the 17th chapter of John) is divided into three parts. First Jesus prays for himself, then for his apostles, then for all who would come to believe in him. Notice how many times the word "glory" is used in today's gospel. Jesus saw his death and resurrection as a moment of glory, a moment when God's saving love would be revealed to the world. He prays that the Father might be glorified in all that was to take place and that in the fulfillment of his mission, he might be a source of life for all who would believe in him. It is comforting to know he prayed for all of us at the Last Supper. He continues to intercede for us each time we celebrate the Lord's Supper.

There is not the time to analyze this prayer thoroughly. My main point today was simply to point out the prayerfulness of Jesus. We see in the first reading how

Jesus followers imitated his example as they gathered together in prayer in the upper room after the Ascension, waiting for the coming of the Holy Spirit.

Louis Evely in his book, *Teach us to Pray*, wrote: "Too many Christians regard God as pilots regard their parachute, namely, good if needed, but better if they can get along without it." We might wonder why would Jesus need to pray? He was already as close to the Father as he possibly could be. I am sure there are many reasons why Jesus prayed, but this question might best be answered with another question: "why do we need to spend time with those who are important to us, with those whom we love?"

A true disciple of our Lord will make prayer a priority in their lives, and by "prayer" I mean more than just a rapidly recited Our Father or Hail Mary. Prayer is spending time with our God. Do we feel like we're too busy? I will never forget what our spiritual director in the seminary told us. The busier we are the more we need to pray.

Today we come together for the greatest prayer there is. As we gather in prayer today, we are not alone and I don't mean simply that there are others here in church with us. Christ is with us and it is in union with his perfect sacrifice of love and obedience on the cross that we offer our prayers and praise to God our Father.

Feast of the Ascension
May 4, 2008

HOMILY – (Acts 1: 1-11, Ephesians 1: 17-23, Matthew 28: 16-20) I will start off with some sad news we received this week. Many of you remember Fr. Stricker who was pastor here before I came. And many of you probably by now are aware that this week he was accused of sexual abuse of a young boy. The event was supposed to have happened back in the 1950's. The alleged victim brought his accusation to the Archdiocese 15 years ago; at that time it was judged to be unsubstantiated. He came forward again a few weeks ago with what the news reported to be new information. This time the case was judged to have a "semblance of truth." That means it looked as if there might be something to it. So according to the Bishop's policy, Fr. Stricker must be put on suspension until the case is resolved. He is no longer living at Little Flower Church and prefers that his new residence not be made public. Although a priest may be suspended, it does not mean he is guilty. In our country a person is presumed innocent until proven guilty. In case a person does have a tendency toward pedophilia, our national Church policy was drawn up in a strict fashion for the protection of others. Because it is so strict, a number of priests who eventually were acquitted had to suffer through a period of suspension. One of them was a classmate of mine, and I know it wasn't easy. This won't be easy for Fr. Stricker either.

I knew Fr. Stricker while I was in the seminary, but I didn't know him well. However, in December, 1990, when I was assigned to St. Patrick's Church here in Northside, I got to know him very well. With the assignment I received, I was told to start the process of merging St. Patrick with St. Boniface. Fr. Stricker and I worked well together, along with parish leaders in both parishes, to make this merger one of the smoothest mergers in the Archdiocese. Once the merger was completed, I became pastor here and Fr. Stricker stayed on for over a year as my associate. I know him as a man with the highest integrity, a man who is deeply spiritual, humble, with a great sense of humor when he gets to know you. He is totally dedicated to serving God and God's people. Since his retirement in 1993 – up until this week when he was put on leave – he has continued his priestly ministry at Little Flower, working as hard as he ever did. During the past 15 years he has continued to come back here weekly to meet with our Legion of Mary as spiritual director. He was just getting ready to celebrate his 60th anniversary as a priest. I know he would appreciate prayers from those who knew him and loved him. At the same time I know him well enough that he would want us to pray also for all victims of abuse.

The feast of the Ascension does not, at first, impress us as a happy event either. Jesus ascended to eternal glory at the right hand of the Father leaving his apostles behind staring into the clouds. However, he did not leave them to fend for themselves without any help. He had promised them the help of the Holy Spirit and he promised them: "I will be with you always." This is a wonderful promise to always remember, in good times and in bad. It is the theme that begins St. Matthew's gospel when he tells us Jesus would be known as Emmanuel, a name that means God is with us. Matthew ends his gospel with the same message.

We like to picture Jesus' ascension exactly the way St. Luke describes it in today's first reading. However, Luke is trying to illustrate a mystery for us, a mystery that is beyond visual perception. To help you understand why I say that, just consider this. The scene St. Luke gives us takes place in Bethany, on the Mount of Olives, just two miles from Jerusalem. Tour guides still point out the exact spot where Jesus supposedly stood. They encourage tourists to use their imagination as they show them his footprint on the rock. The gospel of St. Matthew, which we just heard, tells us Jesus met with his Apostles in Galilee and departed from them there. Does that confuse you? Hopefully, it tells us the ascension is not something that could have been videotaped. It tells us we're dealing with mystery. Certainly Jesus was no longer with his apostles in a visible and tangible way as he was before his crucifixion. Although his physical body had now entered into the glory of heaven, he would still be with his apostles but in a different way. Just to clear up the mystery a little bit, St. Matthew's message seems to be that Jesus met his apostles for the last time in Galilee because Galilee was half pagan. This implied that the message of the gospel is meant for all people. Matthew verbalizes this message too when he quotes Jesus as saying: "Go and make disciples of all nations..."

That would have been a task far greater than any eleven people could accomplish even with help from the Holy Spirit. So, Jesus' words are meant to reach out beyond his first followers to all of us. Jesus wants the message of God's love to reach all people. The job's still not finished.

Let me try to sum up my thoughts on the ascension. The ascension shows us the full glory of the resurrection, sharing in God's glory eternally, a preview of God's plan for all the rest of us who have followed Christ faithfully. The ascension also tells us that Christ is still with us. As he said in the gospel last week, "I will not leave you orphans. I will come to you...The world will no longer see me, but you will see me." Finally, the ascension tells us we have a job to do. We can't spend all our days staring up to the heavens wondering where he's gone, or what he's doing, or what heaven will be like for us. Occasionally it's good to contemplate the next life, it motivates us to live a good life, but we also need to hear what the angels said to the Apostles after Jesus ascended: "Why are you standing there, looking up at the sky?" In effect, I think the angels were saying: "You have a lot of work ahead of you if you're going to make disciples of all nations. You better get with it." Don't forget why the

Mass is called the Mass. It's because the priest used to say at the end: "Ite, missa est," which means "Go, you have been sent." It's our job to bring God's love, which we celebrate in our liturgy, out to the world. Amen.

Pentecost
May 14, 2005

At the vigil we had a baptism:

Today we will have what you might call "a homily in action."

We tend to associate the Holy Spirit with the sacrament of Confirmation and rightly so. The Spirit is given in Confirmation to make us mature and to enable us to witness to our faith. But the Spirit is also present at baptism, just as the Spirit was present at the baptism of Jesus. And you will notice many references to the Spirit in our baptismal service. The Spirit is present uniting us with Christ and giving us a share in God's life.

And so in baptism the Spirit is represented by water. Again we tend to associate the Spirit with fire and this is appropriate for many reasons. But in today's first reading we hear God say he will pour out his Spirit (like a liquid) and in the gospel St. John connects the Spirit with water when he tells us Jesus' statement about living waters flowing from him refer to the Spirit. Water as you know gives life and nothing lives without it. When you see water being poured on the head of little Marissa, think of the Spirit being poured into her, bringing her new life in this sacrament of rebirth.

Pentecost
May 15, 2005

HOMILY – (Acts 2:1-11, 1 Corinthians 12:3b-7, 12-13, John 20:19-23) Pentecost is one of the three most important feasts of the Church year. We know Christmas is one of the three. It's easy to get excited about the birth of a baby, especially when the baby is God's Son and his mother is the Virgin Mary. We know the feast of Jesus' resurrection is the most important feast of all, because if there were no resurrection, we would have no faith or hope at all. But Pentecost, the third most important feast, seems like another ordinary Sunday.

Let me give you a little history of Pentecost. It was not invented by the Church. The Jews were celebrating Pentecost 3000 years ago. It was one of their three most important feasts. It was originally a harvest feast on which the first fruits were offered in gratitude to God. It later came to be celebrated as the anniversary of the giving of the Law to Moses on Mt. Sinai. The word itself means simply 50th, the 50th day after Jewish Passover. The Jews were celebrating that feast when the Spirit came on Jesus' followers. And so Pentecost is still celebrated, but we who are Christians celebrate it as the day on which God sent his Holy Spirit upon the Church.

Pentecost isn't just the celebration of a past event. It is important for us today, because the Holy Spirit is important for us today. The Spirit is hard to picture because the Spirit is within us when we are in God's grace. The Spirit is like the air we breathe, the light that goes on when we have an idea, the fire that burns in our heart. And so the Scriptures use these symbols help us know the Spirit; in the first reading the Spirit is a strong driving wind whereas in John's gospel the Spirit is the gentle breath of Jesus who breathes on his apostles and says "Receive the Holy Spirit." In either case the Spirit is like the air, unable to be seen, but something we cannot live without. The Spirit is like the light that goes on in our mind when we have an idea: Jesus tells us in the gospel "he will guide you to all truth." Jesus couldn't explain everything to the apostles that he wanted them to know, but the Spirit turned on the light in their minds to be able to understand all that he had been teaching them. The Spirit also appeared to the apostles as tongues of fire, a fire that started burning in them to proclaim Christ with courage and conviction.

When we pray, the Spirit is at work in us, helping us to pray. God wants us to know him and love him and the Spirit helps us to do that. But because the Spirit works within us, we are not aware the Spirit is even there. There was a example given by C.S. Lewis about how we grow in knowledge of the universe around us. If we want to know something about rocks, for example, we go and we find rocks. They won't come to us, they won't run away from us. In no way do they cooperate with us in getting to know them. The initiative is all on our side if we are to know rocks. If we want to study wild animals, that's a little different. We have to go find them and then they can run away from us. We have to be very quiet in observing them or they will. The initiative is mostly on our part if we are to know about wild animals, but they can attempt to prevent us from knowing them. If we want to know another human being, and they are determined for us not to know them, we probably won't. We have to win their confidence if they are going to open up to us. The initiative is equally divided: it takes two to make a friendship. When it comes to God, there is no way we could find him or know him if he didn't show himself to us. And he has done so in Jesus Christ. But we cannot not know Jesus

Christ without the help of the Spirit. As Paul tells us in today's second reading: "No one can say Jesus is Lord except in the Holy Spirit." Without the Spirit God is really unknown to us. ..." The Spirit makes us constantly aware of God's presence with us and God's love for us. The Spirit helps the Scriptures come alive for us because through them God speaks to us.

And this relationship with God spills over into everything else we do. And so St. Paul tells us in Galatians: if we live by the Spirit, the Spirit will produce in us love, joy, peace, patience, kindness, goodness, faithfulness, humility, and self-control." Most of us also are familiar with Paul's description of the greatest gift of the Spirit: "I may be able to speak the languages of men and even angels, but if have not love, my speech is no more than a noisy gong or a clanging bell...Love is patient and kind, love is not jealous, etc, etc.

One last point: it was on the Church, that God sent his Spirit. As the first reading tells us Christ followers were all together in one place. And the Spirit gives different gifts to different members of the Church to help each other to know and experience God and God's love. If we want to experience the fullness of the Spirit, we need each other, we need to come together, to worship together, to share our gifts with one another. Without the Spirit we are trying to breathe without air, think without light, love without fire.

Trinity Sunday
May 18, 2008

INTRODUCTION – (Exodus 34:4b-6, 8-9, 2 Corinthians 13:11-13, John 3:16-18) Our basic belief in the Trinity comes out of our attempt to know who Jesus is and to know about the special relationship Jesus has with the Father and with the Spirit who was sent from the Father and the Son. Since our knowledge of Jesus comes from the teaching of the apostles, the gospels and the letters of St. Paul, the fundamental elements of our belief in the Trinity comes from these sources. However, the use of the word "Trinity" to refer to God did not come about until the year 200 AD. It took another 125 years for this doctrine to be formulated in the Nicene Creed which was drawn up at the Council of Nicea in 325 AD. This Creed is the profession of faith which we proclaim each week.

Today in our first reading we hear about Moses who lived 1300 years before Christ. At that time all the nations around him believed in many gods. God's effort at that time to reveal God's self was to try to teach his people that there was no such thing as a multiplicity of gods, but there was only one God. Moses and God's people were to honor and serve this one God only. This is expressed in the first commandment. I am the Lord thy God, thou shalt not have strange gods before me. In our reading today we hear God revealing his sacred name to Moses. In the Hebrew bible, that name is spelled YHWH, but it was never pronounced. That's because the Jews were afraid of taking the slightest risk of using God's sacred name in vain (which the second commandment forbad). So whenever YHWH came up in the text, they always substituted the title "Lord," as we hear in today's first reading. We often associate God in the Old Testament with fire and brimstone, but God's self-revelation to Moses in today's reading is that God is merciful and gracious, slow to anger and rich in kindness and fidelity; characteristics of God that appear also in today's gospel.

HOMILY – From the beginning of recorded history (and long before, I'm sure), human beings have tried to understand the great power that created the world and all that is in it. Nations conceptualized this powerful force in ways they could understand. They pictured gods somewhat like themselves or like animals with divine powers, and they pictured many different gods. The only exception to the practice of worshipping many gods is the Pharaoh Akhenaten, the predecessor to the famous King Tutankhamen. Akhenaten decreed there was only one god, Aten, the sun god. His religion lasted a few years until he died, then the Egyptians went back to their former ways of worshipping Amun, Re, Osiris, etc. I have been listening to a series of lectures about Hinduism, and the lecturer mentioned that in Hindu tradition there are 330 million gods. That would be a job to keep all of them happy. God has made life simple for us in telling us there is only one God we must honor. Even that's too many for some people.

God made it simple for us, but not too simple, for the God we honor is very mysterious, a God we could never have conceived of if it had not been revealed to us. For our God is a God bursting with personality. So much personality, that there are three persons in God, so closely united in being and power and love that there is only one God. And that's the mystery.

As I said earlier, we came to know this mystery through the coming of Jesus, through Jesus' teachings, and the teachings of the apostles. Jesus is God, equal to the Father in every way, but not the same as the Father. The Spirit who comes from the Father and the Son is equal to each of them, and yet not the same as the Father and the Son. Should we be surprised that God is mysterious, that God would be greater than we can understand? If we had a God we could totally understand, wouldn't that be more a God we created out of our own mind, than the God who created us and this entire universe, which also happens to be beyond our ability to fully comprehend.

But, you might ask, what does the idea of the Trinity do for me?

Consider this: when two people are in love with one another they want to know and be known by their lover. God is in love with us. God wants us to know him as much as we are capable and that's why God revealed God's self to us. It's just part of the process of getting to know God better, so we can spend eternity enjoying God's presence and God's love.

Another thing the idea Trinity does for us is it tells us God is not some lonely monarch who needs people around who will entertain him or love him. God is a family who is full of love and fully fulfilled within God's own self. We are loved, not because God is lonely, but because God is so overflowing with love it just pours out to us and we are fulfilled by that love.

Another thing the idea of the Trinity does for us is it helps us know Jesus better. We have the wonderful honor of sharing his life and being one with him through works of charity, prayer and the sacraments, especially the Eucharist.

We reflect we are in God's presence, a mystery to us now, but one day, through our love for him and our fidelity to him we will experience all the love and greatness and beauty of who God is forever. "God so loved the world that he gave his only Son, so that everyone who believes in him might not perish, but might have eternal life." Amen.

Body & Blood of Christ
May 25, 2008

HOMILY – (Deuteronomy 8:2-3, 14b-16a, 1 Corinthians 10:16-17, John 6:51-58) Memorial Day is a testimony to the many women and men who have paid a great price for the freedoms and blessings we enjoy. Memorial Day is also a testimony to our short memories. We need such holidays so we don't forget how much we owe to others. I think one of the worst things we can do for the good of our country and for our own good is to take our blessings for granted. Please do not let Memorial Day get by you without a prayer for those to whom we are indebted for the freedoms and blessings we enjoy; and please do not let the day get by without a sense of gratitude for all we have been given.

Jesus gave us the Mass for the same reason we celebrate Memorial Day – because we can quickly forget how we have been blessed through the sacrifice of Jesus and we quickly forget to be grateful. He told the apostles (and through them, all of us) at the Last Supper: "Do this in memory of me."

Today at Mass we celebrate the feast of the Body and Blood of Christ. Our Mass, though, is more than a simple reminder or remembrance. Our faith teaches us that at Mass we are mystically connected with Christ's sacrifice and with the presence of the Risen Christ. The most ancient document regarding the Eucharist is St. Paul's letter to the Corinthians. As Paul said in today's second reading: "the cup of blessing that we bless, is it not a participation in the blood of Christ? The bread that we break, is it not a participation in the body of Christ?" This word "participation" also means partnership or sharing. It implies a unity with someone or something. The Scriptures and the constant belief of the Church emphasize that this unity with Christ in the Eucharist is not just metaphorical but real. Nowhere is this more clearly spelled out than in the sixth chapter of John's gospel. Our gospel today was a portion of that chapter. Jesus said "the bread that I will give is my flesh for the life of the world...." He went on to say: "unless you eat the flesh of the Son of Man and drink his blood, you do not have life within you." The bread and wine truly become the risen Christ. When we receive him we become so united with him that we share in his risen, divine life. How do we know this? Right now, we know it only because he told us so. St. John tells us Jesus lost many of his followers over this issue. They said it was crazy talk and walked away. Jesus didn't call them back and say, "you misunderstood me, or I'm just talking symbolically." He just turned to the apostles and said, "are you going to leave me too?" Peter spoke up and said, "where are we going to go. We have come to believe and are convinced you are the Holy One of God." It takes faith to say that. It's the kind of faith it takes to approach the Eucharist. Some day when we've left this life and find ourselves in the next life, then we will know that we have been fed with food that gave us eternal life.

I find it interesting that in John's gospel the word "flesh" is used instead of "body," as in "this is my body,' which the wording the other gospels use. The word "body" is more abstract, whereas "flesh" is more concrete; it conjures up images of bone and muscle and tendons and skin. In John's gospel Jesus is telling us when he gives us himself to eat, it is really his body, not just some abstract concept. The appearance, the taste, the feel and color remain as bread and wine, so we can make him our food and drink for eternal life.

It is interesting that so many people believe the Son of God became human but cannot become bread and wine. At Christmas our churches are full and we celebrate the birth of Jesus, the Son of God who became a little baby in order to share our life. Yet, some of the same people have difficulty believing God cannot become bread and wine. When I try to picture this, I realize that the nature of God is as far from us as the most distant galaxy, while it's relatively just a short hop, skip and a jump between being human and being bread and wine which is made up of the same stuff we are. For those who do believe in the mystery and the miracle, however, the biggest danger is for the believer to lose their sense of awe because the Eucharist has been made so easily available to us.

There are many ways to approach today's mystery. One of my favorite ways is to think of it in terms of energy. Think of an acorn and an acorn sized stone. They might look similar, but one is full of life ready to break out and grow into a tree, and the other will never do anything but be a stone. One has the energy of life within it and the other does not. We look at the host. It doesn't look any different after the consecration than it did before, but a whole new energy replaced what was there before: a divine energy that promises: "Whoever eats this bread will live forever." Eating healthy food calls for discipline. It's so easy and convenient to fill our bodies with junk. Jesus is giving us something healthy, but it requires more discipline on Saturday evening or Sunday morning to get to Church than it does to laying in bed or watching TV or to go to some sporting event.

In today's feast the Church reminds us of the great gift Christ has given us, himself. What greater gift of love can a person give than their own selves? May we not take it for granted!

10th Sunday in Ordinary Time
June 8, 2008

INTRODUCTION – (Hosea 6:3-6, Romans 4:18-25, Matthew 9:9-13) Today's first reading is very confusing unless you know it is made up of two parts. In the first part the Prophet quotes from a Jewish prayer in which the people assure themselves of God's love and mercy. The second part that begins with the words "What can I do with you, Ephraim" indicates the shallowness of their prayer, for there was little sign of their love for God and for one another. Thus their sacrifices and prayers were without meaning. The psalm that follows echoes this theme.

HOMILY – One time a reporter asked the notorious bank robber, Willie Sutton, why he kept robbing banks. He answered, "Because that's where the money is." Jesus was asked why he hung out with sinners and ate with them? That's where he would find the people who needed salvation. It's not as if the self-righteous people like the Pharisees didn't need to be saved. It's just that they thought they didn't need to hear Jesus' message of forgiveness for they considered themselves already perfect. The image the gospel gives me is Jesus going out looking for people who will respond to him and Matthew did. We are always in need of his help and he continues to reach out to us through his Spirit, his Word and his sacraments.

Every year we have a speaker come to us to speak to us about the missions, to make us aware that our church is not just St. Boniface but it is worldwide. With our prayers and financial support we can help those who reach out to other parts of the world to bring God's message of love and salvation to those without faith. Ms Julie Lupien will speak to us at the end of Mass about the unique work she does in the area of mission work. Please stay to give her a few minutes of your time to hear what she has to say and please help her in her work to whatever extent you can. There is a special envelope in the pews you can use as your response to her appeal. Please do not use the envelope until after she has a chance to talk to us and then bring it back with you next week or mail it in.

11th Sunday in Ordinary Time
June 15, 2008

INTRODUCTION – (Exodus 19:2-6a, Romans 5:6-11, Matthew 9:36-10:8) Our first reading takes us back to the time right after Moses had led God's people out of Egypt. God was beginning to make a covenant with them. As the covenant began, God reminded them of what he had done for them and the special relationship they would have with him if they would keep his covenant.

Our psalm refrain reminds us we are his people today and, through fidelity to our covenant with him, we will enjoy God's kindness and faithfulness forever.

The second reading is one of my very favorites. It tells us that even while we were sinners, lacking in grace, God loved us. Now that we share his life, how much more can we be sure of his love!

HOMILY – Here are a few things you will never hear fathers say:

1) Well, what do you know, I'm lost. It looks like I'll have to stop and ask for directions.

2) Here's a credit card and the keys to my new car – go crazy!

3) Your mother and I are going away for the weekend – it would be a good opportunity for you to have a party.

4) No son of mine is going to live under my roof without an earring – now quit complaining about it and lets go to the mall to get one.

5) Why do you want to go and get a job this summer? I make plenty of money for you to spend.

6) Father's Day? Aahh – don't worry about that – it's no big deal!

Happy Father's Day to all who nurture and guide others to success in this life and into the next.

Jesus' father-like love for us is demonstrated in today's gospel. He had pity for the crowds. The Greek word here for "pity" is a mouthful: σπλαγχνίζομαι. It's the word that gives us the English word: spleen. It means Jesus was emotionally moved in the depths of his being. The people had no leadership. They were suffering. They were like sheep without a shepherd. Here was the One who could give them direction and healing. But he needed help. Too many people were in need. So he chose twelve among his followers who would work closely with him, bringing encouragement to the hopeless, freedom to those whose lives were controlled by evil, healing to those broken down by disease. All they needed was to open their hearts and minds in faith to the message of Jesus.

Jesus is the real healer, the only savior, our source of hope and life and holiness. When the gospel tells us he gave authority to the twelve, it was the authority to act in his name and by his power. Whenever one who has been delegated is acting in his name, it is really Jesus who is present and is at work. I say this all the time whenever I do a baptism. I don't have power personally to give divine life to an infant. I have the authority to do so because it was given to me, but it is Christ in whose name I serve. It is Christ who is really doing it. I always illustrate this with the gospel of Jesus healing a blind man by putting mud on the man's eyes. The mud brought healing because of the action of Jesus and the faith of the man who was blind. When I baptize, I tell people I'm kind of like the mud. Jesus is just using me to do what he wants to do: bring light and life to the one being baptized. St. Augustine illustrated this idea in a dramatic way by saying it wouldn't matter if St. Peter were here doing the baptism, or St. Paul or Judas; it is Christ who is baptizing.

This principal that the sacraments are the actions of Christ carries through all the sacraments. It is Christ who forgives sins in the sacrament of reconciliation speaking through the words of the priest; it is Christ who is the great high priest offering acceptable sacrifice to the Father at Mass. That's one of the things that makes the Mass so special. It's not just our private prayer. It is our sacrifice of thanksgiving offered to the Father in union with Jesus' sacrifice of himself. He is both the priest and the victim and we are blest to share in this perfect sacrifice. It is Christ who gives the Spirit in confirmation, Christ who unites a man and woman in marriage to grow in love and to share in the work of creation by bringing new life into the world. It is Christ who ordains deacons, priests and bishops to serve God's people in his name. It is Christ who touches us with his healing love in the sacrament of the sick.

Today we hear about Jesus' pity, his σπλαγχνίζομαι, a word without a good English translation. He had deep feelings for those who suffer and that's why he gave us the sacrament of the sick. St. Mark tells us specifically, and St. James too, that oil is to be used in this healing.

Of course, God expects us to use whatever gifts he has given us to find healing: a healthy diet, exercise, a good doctor, etc. Prayer is one of those gifts and should be used in combination with whatever resources we have and should not just be a last resort. "I guess all we can do is pray." It may be a last resort, but it should be a first resort too. I anoint practically everyone I visit in the hospital. I believe in the power of this sacrament. The primary purpose of the sacrament is for sickness and only secondarily does it prepare a person for death. I thought that today's gospel would be a good lead into the sacrament of the sick which I will offer after Mass today. Let's pray it will bring healing to those who seek it.

12th Sunday in Ordinary Time
June 22, 2008

INTRODUCTION – (Jeremiah 20: 10-13, Romans 5: 12-15, Matthew 10: 26-33) The prophet, Jeremiah lived in Israel about 600 years before Christ. The Babylonian destruction of Israel was immanent. The Babylonians came from modern day Iraq. Their capital, Babylon, was located just 100 miles south of Baghdad. Jeremiah was warning God's people that they could avoid the destruction that was on its way if they started living according to God's laws (most of which were being flagrantly ignored or violated. The people didn't like the message, so they decided to kill Jeremiah. His words in today's first reading reflect the pain and misery he experienced for being faithful to his mission. We should not be shocked when we hear him pray that God take vengeance on his persecutors. After all, he was human and not as perfect as Jesus who was able to pray for those who crucified him.

Our first reading leads into the gospel. As we heard last Sunday, Jesus had just chosen his twelve apostles. In today's gospel he prepares to send them out as missionaries. He is warning them their message will not always be well received, they may even suffer and die for it, but they must preach with courage and not be afraid of what might happen to them if they meet rejection.

HOMILY – Pope John Paul II had as his motto: "Be not afraid." Of course, he was quoting our Lord whom we just heard give the same mandate to his apostles in today's gospel, "Do not be afraid." Since God knows how many hairs are on our head and is aware when even a little sparrow dies, then he's aware of every detail of our own lives. Although he is aware, and cares, he does not guarantee us that bad things will not happen to us. Ups and downs are part of our existence and they even happened to God's holy prophets and to Jesus himself. Because God is aware and he cares he tells us not to fear, for he is in control and will make everything turn out right for those who are faithful to him.

"Be not afraid." Sometimes that's easier said than done. Fear is built into us and we feel it when we feel threatened. If fear were not a part of our nature, we wouldn't even exist today, because long ago our ancestors would not have had sense to get out of the way of charging wild animals, saber tooth tigers or poisonous snakes. Nor would we be moved to get out of the way of cars and trucks coming at us 50 miles an hour. Fear enables us to survive, to know when to fight, to know when to run. But sometimes it gets out of control and takes over our life, whether that fear comes from a real threat or an imagined one. Faith is a big help to deal with fear, and sharing our fears with a trusted friend can be helpful, but sometimes fear is so controlling that counseling or medication is required.

I think when Jesus tells us not to fear, he's not talking about the spontaneous reaction we feel when we are threatened, he's telling us not to worry and to put our trust in him that things will come out alright in the end. The words of St. Paul, "We know that all things work for good for those who love God" (Rom 8,28), have been a constant help to me to stay together during very trying times. One thing Jesus does tell us to fear is God! "Do not be afraid of those who can kill the body but cannot kill the soul; rather, be afraid of the one who can destroy both soul and body in Gehenna." In Old Testament times Gehenna was a place of human sacrifice to pagan idols. At the time of Jesus it was a garbage dump, which was constantly burning. Thus Gehenna became the symbol of evil and hell. Jesus' words confuse some people! Aren't we supposed to love God, but if we fear him, how can we love him? Doesn't St. John tell us "perfect love casts out fear?" All of that is true. For those who have a "reward and punishment" view of life, a little fear might help them stay on the straight and narrow. For those who have moved beyond the "reward and punishment" stage, this fear that Jesus talks about is the fear of being unfaithful to God or having a sense of awe, respect and reverence when we approach God. Those who fear God in this way will approach him with awe, respect and reverence frequently. In either case, a little healthy fear of God will greatly reduce our fear of other things in life, including death itself.

I know from many years of dealing with people that if we are at peace with God and know the Lord is with us, there will be fewer things in life that can upset us or frighten us. Amen.

13th Sunday in Ordinary Time
June 26, 2005

INTRODUCTION – (2 Kgs 4:8-11, 14-16a, Rom 6:3-4, 8-11, Matt 10:37-42) In our gospel today Jesus tells us we must die to ourselves: "Whoever loses his life for my sake will find it." Today's second reading from Paul tells us that through baptism we have died with Christ and rose with him to share in his divine life. Paul was making reference to the normal way baptism was administered in his day. A person was dunked in the water, symbolizing death and burial and then brought out of the water, symbolizing a resurrection. A person does not have to be baptized by immersion to experience the spiritual effects of the sacrament, namely dying to selfishness and sin and beginning a new life in Christ.

There is a second theme in today's readings: that of kindness to God's holy ones. Jesus is about to send his apostles out as missionaries and he promises them anyone who does a simple act of kindness for them will not lose their reward. In those days there were not hotels and motels. Travelers had to depend on the kindness of others when they traveled. The prophet Elisha in our first reading lived about 800 years before Christ. He often traveled to Mt. Carmel to pray and on his journey to Mt. Carmel he regularly stopped to stay at the home of a couple who lived in a town nearby. The story emphasizes the importance to being receptive to those sent to us by God, whether they be prophets or apostles. The story also shows that if one is kind to one sent by God, God will not let us outdo him in generosity.

HOMILY – We heard Jesus tell us not to let anything or anyone (even those who are closest to us, even our own lives) be more important than he is. He does not make this request for his own glorification. He isn't looking for worldly glory. His life was a life of poverty and simplicity. Besides he has all the glory he needs. He is, after all, Son of God. You can't get any higher than that. He asks us to give him central place in our hearts and in our lives for our own sake and for our own happiness. We'll never really be satisfied in life until we possess and are fully possessed by the life that Christ came to bring us. As St. Augustine said, "Thou hast made us for thyself O Lord and our hearts are restless until they rest in thee."

There are two themes that flow from this basic truth. I think the first message is that the gospel is not always a "feel good" message. Some people only want to hear peace, love and joy when they come to Church. They want a Church that always makes them "feel good." Peace, love and joy are wonderful and Jesus' promises of lasting happiness fill us with hope, and all preachers love to preach about these things, but sometimes, like today, the gospel message is not easy to hear. Being willing to give up everything for Christ, even our own lives (and many people did), is a hard message. Dietrich Bonhoeffer, a Lutheran minister who spent the last two years of his life in prison for resisting Hitler, wrote a lot about "cheap grace," grace that didn't cost us much. Cheap grace means hoping to gain eternal happiness while asking ourselves, "What is the least I can get by with." One of Bonhoeffer's most memorable lines is "When Christ calls a person, he bids him come and die." Following Christ can cost us dearly. If we're afraid of that, if we're always looking for a Church that doesn't really challenge us, then we are not wanting to hear Christ.

The second theme of today's gospel is kindness, especially to those who bring this message of life through death to us. That includes our hierarchy, the priests and religious, but it includes parents and grandparents, neighbors and friends, teachers and spouses and all who have taught us about Christ and who have been models of faith for us. Most of us didn't get our faith out of a textbook. We got it by God's inspiration and by seeing how others lived it. I did come to know some wonderful priests when I was growing up, but most seemed to me to be stuffy and distant. My faith came primarily from my parents and those who taught me in school. And it still is enriched by people I have known and do know now at St. Boniface. When you are here faithfully every week and you pray and sing from your hearts, my spirits are lifted in prayer. So this act of kindness to God's messengers that Jesus promises to reward applies to anyone. A young girl told the story about needing to have her teeth repaired when she was in college. Being a struggling college student, she could hardly afford to have one tooth filled, but the pain was so bad she had to see a dentist. When she went, he wanted to fix all her teeth and she said I can't afford it and started to leave. He understood and said "well, when you finish college you'll get a job and make some money and you can pay me then." He did the job, on credit, and it made a wonderful difference in the way she felt. She was able to pay him off after graduation. She called him a "woodwork angel." She described "woodwork angels" as strangers who come out of nowhere, out of the woodwork, when a person needs help. They may help out with money, skills, protection from danger or from making a big mistake, they may offer us hospitality as the woman did for the prophet Elisha or they may simply offer us a cup of cold water. We all need them. We all need to be one to others. Herman Melville said, "We cannot live only for ourselves. A thousand fibers connect us with our fellow human beings." And Elbert Hubbard said, "People are rich only as they give. He who gives great service gets great returns." Jesus said, "whoever gives only a cup of cold water to one of these little ones to drink because the little one is a disciple – amen, I say to you, he will surely not lose his reward."

Feast of St. Peter & St. Paul
June 29, 2008

INTRODUCTION – (Acts 12: 1-11, 2 Timothy 4: 6-8, 17-18, Matthew 16; 13-19) At 4:00 Mass:

Christ continues to feed and guide his people through the apostles. We see today how he does this through two of them, Peter and Paul. Peter, in today's first reading, shows us Jesus at work through him and John in healing a person crippled from birth. Peter's position as leader and chief shepherd of God's people is recognized in today's gospel. This was written long after Peter had been put to death, so it is not just Peter who is appointed chief shepherd, but those who would succeed him. We hear from St. Paul in the second reading. Paul was a powerful teacher and his mission was, to a large part, to the Gentiles. He recognized that fidelity to Christ did not require Gentiles to observe all of Jewish law with its feasts and rituals and sacrifices and dietary requirements. In today's second reading he is assuring his readers that he teaches with divine authority and has received backing from Peter (Cephas) and the other leaders of the early Church.

At Sunday Masses:

A society cannot survive without structure, organization and authority. Today's feast of the apostles, Peter and Paul, especially today's gospel, reminds us of the way Christ structured his Church with Peter as the head. When we hear this gospel, it might be worth knowing that it was written after Peter had already been put to death. St. Matthew wants us to know that it was a leadership position Jesus was creating when he made Peter the rock and gave him the keys of the kingdom. It was not just a personal prerogative of Peter's. If it were personal only to Peter, who was dead by the time Matthew was writing, why would St. Matthew have made so much of it in his gospel?

I would like you to notice also in today's readings the theme of God helping those who put their trust in him. The first reading tells us how God rescued Peter from prison. The psalm that follows is the prayer of a person praising God for rescuing them from fear and danger. We could easily imagine Peter praying this psalm as he left prison. In the second reading Paul realizes he is approaching the end of his life and he praises God for all the ways he has been protected during his ministry.

HOMILY – Today we celebrate the feast of Saints Peter and Paul. It is a very ancient feast going back to around the year 250 A.D. The two are honored because they are the two apostles about whom we know the most. They were the greatest influence on the Church at its beginning. Tradition has it they died together in Rome during the persecution of the Emperor Nero. Most historians suspect that Nero himself started the fire that burned most of Rome in order to clear out old houses and buildings to make room for his own ambitious building projects. Then he blamed the fire on the Christians in order to take suspicion off himself.

Peter was crucified upside down, again tradition has it that he did not consider himself worthy of dying in the same way his Master had died. Paul was beheaded. Although he was a Jew, he also was legally, by birth, a Roman citizen. Roman law decreed that Roman citizens could not be crucified because it was such a horrific way to die and being exempt from crucifixion was one of the perks of being a Roman citizen.

This year the spotlight is on St. Paul because the Holy Father proclaimed that the rest of this year and the first six months of next year be a year in honor of St. Paul. No one knows when he was born exactly, but scholars figure it was roughly 2000 years ago (give or take three or four years). So we are celebrating his 2000th birthday as closely as we can figure it.

We don't know if Paul ever saw Jesus in the flesh. Paul was born in Tarsus, a city in Asia Minor, which is now modern day Turkey. He spoke Greek and Aramaic and wrote all of his letters in Greek. He was a Pharisee and 1000 % dedicated to observance of Jewish law and traditions. Sometime after the death and resurrection of Jesus, he began persecuting the early followers of Christ. He was present at the martyrdom of St. Steven, the first martyr. He viewed those who believed in Jesus as heretics. He was such a zealous devotee to the Jewish Law that he would go looking for believers in Jesus to arrest them and prosecute them. It was on such a journey to Damascus that the Risen Christ spoke to Paul. Paul was enveloped in a bright light and fell to the ground. There is no mention of a horse, although people are used to saying he was thrown off his horse. This idea came from a painting of the event. I rather believe Paul was walking or riding a donkey, which was the usual means of transportation. He heard someone call him, and when he asked who was calling him, Jesus answered: "I am Jesus whom you are persecuting." Then Jesus said: "Now get up and go into the city and you will be told what you must do." Paul got up but he was a new man. He was ill and blind for a few days until he was healed by one of Jesus' followers and was baptized. In his encounter with Jesus, he discovered Jesus was not a heretic and condemned criminal, but the glorified Lord who has risen from the dead and lives in his Church. He would learn that his mission would be to the Gentiles and that the good news Jesus proclaimed was to be preached to all people. This is when Paul became an Apostle for the word Apostle means one who has been sent. He would come to understand how we are saved by Jesus' death and resurrection and by our incorporation into this saving event through three things: 1) faith, 2) the sacraments, especially baptism and the Eucharist and 3) our love for one another.

Paul wrote more than any other New Testament author. One could keep on talking about him because he wrote so much. There is an insert in today's bulletin that says more about Paul. But to put everything succinctly, Paul's life and mission can be summed up in the one sentence Jesus spoke to him on the way to Damascus: "I am Jesus whom you are persecuting."

As I conclude, we might recall the most famous lines Paul wrote: "love is kind, love is patient, love is not jealous, it is not pompous, etc." ending with the sentence: "love never fails." The kind of love Paul talks about is a love that is rooted in Christ. We express that love as we gather here in faith today, giving God our time and worship and praying for one another. May we continue to express that same love for one another throughout the coming week.

14th Sunday in Ordinary Time
July 6, 2008

INTRODUCTION – (Zechariah 9: 9-10, Romans 8: 9, 11-13, Matthew 11: 25-30) Three hundred years is a long time. In our nation, three hundred years would take us back to before George Washington was born and long before our Declaration of Independence. In our first reading we hear from Zechariah the prophet. For those who first heard Zechariah's words, there would have been the realization that it had been three hundred years since their country had a king and had known independence. They could recall their sad history that three hundred years earlier their homes and lands, their city and their Temple had been destroyed and they were exiled to Babylon and became Babylonian slaves. Then the Persians conquered the Babylonians, allowed the Jews to return home, but continued to rule them and to collect taxes from those they ruled. Then came the Greeks who conquered Israel and who eventually bitterly persecuted Jews who would not give up their faith and their traditions. So when the prophet Zechariah tells God's people, "Rejoice!" many of them probably thought he had been out in the sun far too long. But God's prophet has reason to be full of joy. The role of a prophet is to see clearly what others cannot see. He could see a time when there would be no more war, or exile, destruction or conquest. He could see that one day they would have their own king, a king who would bring peace. That is the symbol of the donkey in the first reading. Horses were weapons of war, used by warriors and conquerors. Horses, chariots, warriors' bows and other instruments of war would be outlawed in his kingdom. The people of Jerusalem remembered this prophecy when Jesus came riding into Jerusalem on a donkey on Palm Sunday. We're not at Palm Sunday yet. But we hear in today's gospel Jesus reveals himself as a man of peace who is meek and humble of heart. That's why the passage from Zechariah was chosen for our first reading. Someday after we learn to better follow Jesus, the man of peace, maybe we will then see Zechariah's prophecy of peace fully fulfilled.

HOMILY – Up until a few hundred years ago, the yoke was very common. It would join two animals together so their combined strength could pull a plow or wagon. Now we have trucks and tractors to do the work of animals. The word yoke also had a symbolic meaning. It symbolized slavery and servitude.

At the time of Jesus, the Jewish law sometimes was referred to as a yoke, a burden to be endured. The way the Scribes and Pharisees interpreted God's law certainly proved to be a burden on God's people. (Mt. 23,4) When Jesus said, "take my yoke upon you and learn from me," he was contrasting his way, his teachings to the Jewish leaders' incorrect and burdensome interpretations of God's law that the people would hear weekly in their synagogues. The spirit behind Jesus' teachings would lift their burdens and be refreshing. "Come to me all you who labor and are burdened and I will give you rest."

I think there are two ideas that are worth reflecting on. 1) Jesus said "my yoke is easy and my burden light." Every law is a burden, and this includes even the laws Jesus gave us, for law involves obligations and responsibilities, things we have to do and obey. When we obey his law, we discover it is not overburdening, rather it will lift our spirits and will lead us to eternal life. Sin, which is another word for disobedience to God, puts a burden on us. St. Paul tells us when we sin we become indebted to sin. We all know what debt can do to us. It weighs us down. Next week Paul will tell us more about how sin can enslave us, while living according to the Spirit gives us life.

This past week we celebrated our Independence Day. But there's no independence from God. We treasure our freedom in this country, but if we think freedom is doing anything we want, we won't have any freedom at all. I think the image of a sailboat is a good example of what I'm saying. I used to sail a lot. It was important that you kept your hand on the tiller and kept the sail at the right angle to the wind. If you let the boat go free, it would be a disaster. Many times I turned wrong into the wind and got blown over. Once, on a really cold, windy day, I spent a couple of hours in very cold water before someone rescued me. I never told this story before because having to be rescued is embarrassing for a sailor. In our own lives we need to keep going in the right direction to find peace and happiness, and God's laws are meant to keep us going in that direction. God's way is not to limit our freedom as sometimes people think, but to guide us to peace and happiness. When we ignore or violate his law (which is sin) we become a slave to our own worst selves.

2) The other thing about a yoke is that it joins two animals together. With a yoke, one animal does not pull the wagon or the plow alone. When Jesus said, "come to me…take my yoke upon you," he is offering to be our partner in bearing our burdens. He is telling us we won't go through life alone. He promised at the Last Supper he would not leave us orphans (Jn. 14,18) All we need to do, and sometimes we need to do it every day, is to commit ourselves to following him and he will be there for us. We can be sure of that! Amen.

15th Sunday in Ordinary Time
July 13, 2008

INTRODUCTION – (Isaiah 55: 10-11, Romans 8: 18-23, Matthew 13: 1-23) The prophet, whom we hear in today's first reading, was speaking to God's captive people in Babylon. Through the prophet, God is telling them they would soon be able to return home. Their exile, which lasted 50 years, was suddenly at an end. No doubt this seemed like an impossibility. God assures them his promise will be fulfilled. God said his word is like the rain. When God sends the rain it does the work of keeping the world green and alive. When God sends out his word, it is not full of empty promises, but it has the power to be effective.

HOMILY – Today we have a choice as to whether to do the long form or short form of the gospel. I chose the short form, because I believe most of us already know that Jesus was the one who scattered the seed by speaking God's word to all who would listen. Not everyone responded in the same way. Some ignored him, some received his message with enthusiasm but quickly forgot or was easily distracted. Some took God's word to heart and grew in God's grace and love. God's word was generously offered to all people, but not everyone benefited from it. Another purpose Jesus may have had in telling this parable was to help his apostles understand why everyone did not follow Jesus with as much excitement as they did.

It is a parable so rich in meaning that it has other interpretations as well. I came across a delightful story by Megan McKenna in her book: *Parables: the Arrows of God* which might give us another way of looking at today's parable.

There was a woman who was depressed over the state of the world. She longed for love among her family and friends, peace among all people, compassion for the poor and vulnerable. There were problems everywhere as she saw so much selfishness, greed, hatred, lack of moral values.

One day she came upon a little shop. She walked in and was surprised to see someone behind the counter who reminded her of Jesus. She couldn't believe it really was Jesus, but the similarity was so striking that she just had to go to him and ask: "Excuse me, are you Jesus?" "I am." "Do you work here?" "No, I am the owner." "What do you sell here?" "Well, I really don't sell anything. It's all free. I have here just about anything you might want. You're welcome to walk around the aisles and see what you might be interested in. Make a list of all the things you want and bring it back to me. I'll see what I can do for you." She was amazed at what she saw on the shelves: peace on earth, food to feed the hungry, clean air and water, warm clothing for the poor, forgiveness. The woman compiled a long list and brought it back to Jesus. When Jesus looked at all the items she had written down he smiled and said "no problem." He bent down behind the counter and ran his fingers through several boxes. He then stood up and laid out a series of small envelopes for the woman. "What are these?" she asked. "Seed packets," Jesus replied. "This is a catalogue store." "You mean I don't get the finished product?" she asked. "No," Jesus said. "Just take these seeds home, plant them and nurture them and help them grow and you will be quite pleased with the results." She said "Oh!" and left the store without taking anything with her. Most of us want God to solve problems for us overnight, and when he does that's great, but mostly he gives us the means and the help we need and calls us to have faith and patience. Live by God's word, it will not disappoint us. As God promised in today's first reading: "my word will not return to me void, but shall do my will, achieving the end for which I sent it."

16th Sunday in Ordinary Time
July 20, 2008

INTRODUCTION – (Wisdom 12: 13, 16-19, Romans 8: 26-27, Matthew 13: 24-43) The first reading today could be difficult to follow. It is from the book of Wisdom, a book of the bible written about 100 years before Christ. At this time, the Jews were being persecuted for their faith. Many Jews were giving up their belief in God and going over to pagan ways. The author of this book is struggling with the question: "why is God allowing this evil to go on?" His conclusion is that God's power is not directed toward evil people, but it shows itself in God's patience, wanting people to repent and allowing them time to do so. This theme prepares us for the gospel, which also deals with the problem of evil.

HOMILY – I'll start with the parable of the wheat and the weeds. A few months ago I had a conversation with a professed atheist. He was convinced that God could not exist because there was so much evil in the world. I wasn't able to convince him otherwise. He was like the farm workers in today's gospel who wanted to go out into the field and pull up all the weeds. No one who tries to grow a garden lets the weeds grow along with the flowers and vegetables they plant, but as with many of Jesus' parables, God does exactly what we would not expect. The owner of the farm, who represents God, said let the wheat and weeds grow together and we'll separate them at harvest time. Because God does not always do things the way we think he should, many people often get angry with God or turn away altogether. They forget who's the Master.

Thank God who is so patient, or there might be a mighty small population in today's world. If any of us think we're the ones God would not pluck up, then you can sign up after Mass to begin your canonization process. Other than the Blessed Virgin and Jesus himself, we're all sinners and in need of salvation. I personally am most grateful that God is patient with me.

Although we admit we all fail to be as holy as we know we should be, and we know God is patient and merciful, this is not the time to beat ourselves up. This is a time to be grateful for his way of dealing with us stems from his infinite love for us. That is the deeper mystery. God delights in us, even though we have weeds growing in our garden. He gives us his help to continue growing in holiness. This idea connects with the other two parables about the mustard seed and the yeast, for growth is a slow process.

Of course these two parables are originally meant to describe the kingdom that God is establishing through the ministry of Jesus Christ, a kingdom that started with a very tiny group of followers and continues to grow. I'll bet the apostles would never have imagined that it would still be growing 2000 years later and would number 2 billion followers of Christ (if you include in that number all Christian denominations).

However, we can see these two parables from a personal perspective in that, although we want to love and serve God, we do not become perfect overnight. We must be patient with ourselves for growth takes much longer than we want it to at times. It will happen if we keep doing the best we can to pray and to do what God wants. St. Paul's letter to the Romans is apropos when he tells us in today's second reading we do not know how to pray as we ought, so the Holy Spirit helps us in our prayers by interceding for us.

That points out what is so unique about the Mass. The Mass is the greatest, and as Jesus said, the most powerful way to pray. We are joined together in prayer. The Mass is also great because it is the prayer and perfect sacrifice of Jesus, and we get to join our prayer and worship with his. There are lots of wonderful and powerful prayers and the Holy Spirit helps us in our prayers. Most of all the Spirit is with us now as we thank God for his goodness to us and ask his blessing upon us.

17th Sunday in Ordinary Time
July 27, 2008

INTRODUCTION – (1 Kings 3: 5,7-12, Romans 8: 28-30, Matthew 13: 44-52) King David died about 970 years before Christ. His son, Solomon, succeeded him as king of Israel. Today's first reading is Solomon's prayer as he begins his reign. He prayed for an understanding heart that he would reign well. Of all the gifts he could have asked for, he valued wisdom more than anything else. God's commands guide us to wisdom, so in the psalm refrain we praise God for this gift.

HOMILY – Again this Sunday we hear Jesus teaching us about the kingdom of heaven. The parable about the net thrown in the sea was explained and the first two parables about the treasure and the pearl are pretty obvious. However, I have a story that will help us think more deeply about the idea of a treasure.

A lady wrote this story about herself. She recalled that when she was a child her wealthy parents would take an extended vacation every summer and they would leave their child in the care of a sitter. When the girl was eleven, the sitter quit right before the parents were to go on vacation, but the parents were able to hire a substitute. The girl came upon her mother wrapping up and hiding all the family jewels and silverware. The little girl asked why, since her mother had never done that before. Her mother explained she could not trust the new sitter with the family valuables. You can imagine how the little girl interpreted this remark. The parents were trusting the sitter with their daughter but not with anything that had material value. Was she not a "family valuable" of greater importance than knives and forks?

That remark did not make the little girl feel valued. I am sure her parents would have protested that they greatly valued their daughter. The point I am making is that we can all say we value something or someone. But sometimes the things or people we value most are taken for granted.

Jesus is telling us today that the kingdom of God and living in God's good grace is of the highest value to us. Going to Mass, prayer, keeping the Commandments, loving God and each other is not just a form of insurance that we will be happy in the next life. It is something that we make part of our lives. The man who found the treasure was lucky, but the treasure wasn't legally and fully his until he sacrificed his possessions in order to buy the field. The man who wanted the pearl had to do the same. The kingdom of heaven doesn't come automatically. We have to invest in it to really possess it, or rather I should say, to have it possess us. The most important thing we have to invest is our time, time to pray and to reflect on the Scriptures, perhaps even to serve God or the Church with some of our gifts and talents. But it also requires an investment of our will, choosing to guide our lives by Christ's teachings rather than making up our own rules about what's good or bad. It even takes an investment of our finances, since if we value our faith, we will adequately support it.

When this life is over, we will have to leave behind most of our treasures. But we will take with us our good works and our love for God and others; these will be our joy for all eternity. A life of holiness and goodness is a treasure that will not fail. Amen.

18th Sunday in Ordinary Time
August 3, 2008

INTRODUCTION – (Isaiah 55:1-3, Romans 8:35, 37-39, Matthew 14:13-21) Today's first reading sounds like an invitation to a summer picnic. But it is not. The prophet was speaking to God's people who were captives and exiles in Babylon over 500 years before Christ, announcing that their captivity was ended. God was getting ready to bring them back home. The rich and abundant food mentioned in this reading symbolized the blessings they would soon enjoy. Those who come to receive God's blessings will be satisfied beyond their wildest dreams and those who come to him would receive these blessings free of charge. Notice how often the word "come" is used. Too often we allow temptation to lead us away from God, looking for happiness and satisfaction in the wrong places only to end up paying dearly for something that was worth little or nothing. If the food mentioned here sounds pretty common and ordinary, I'm sure some of the foods mentioned were luxuries for an exiled and enslaved people! Our first reading is meant to prepare us for the gospel where Jesus feeds a multitude in a miraculous way.

HOMILY – There was a minister who began his sermon every Sunday by first bowing his head for a moment of prayer. One day his little daughter asked him why he did that. He was pleased that his daughter noticed this gesture of prayer he started with and he told her "I ask God to help me preach a good sermon." Then she said, "Then why doesn't he help you do it?" Notice, I never bow my head before I preach for fear some one might say that to me some day!

Seriously though, the little girl found out God doesn't

always give us everything we ask for. But in today's first reading he tells us he will give us what we truly need if we come to him. In the gospel we hear how Jesus responded to the needs of the people who came to him.

St. Matthew describes Jesus feeding the people by telling us: "he took bread, said the blessing, broke the loaves and gave them to the disciples." The connection with the Eucharist is obvious and deliberate. As St. Matthew tells us about the miracle of the loaves and fishes, he wants us to be aware of how Jesus feeds us in a miraculous way in the Eucharist.

There was an article in the Catholic Telegraph this past week describing a study of Catholics in Britain. I'm sure it's the same on this side of the Atlantic Ocean. The study said many Catholics are getting away from regular Mass attendance and the sacraments because of the high stress in their lives. They are exhausted by the end of the week with all the demands of home and job, and Church is just one more thing to do and the easiest thing to skip. The report said "Families who do go to Mass regularly are making tremendous sacrifices to do so."

And yet, this is where we will best find the strength and help we need to cope and to survive. Jesus promises it to us. Research has shown that, in general, those who attend Church regularly live happier and more successful lives. It is natural for us to think of Jesus feeding us when we go to Holy Communion. For he feeds us then with his own body and blood. But another way he feeds us that we may not think of is with his word. He tells us in the first reading: "come to me heedfully," in other words come alert and attentively. He tells us "listen, that you may have life."

Before Jesus feeds us with himself in Communion, he feeds our minds and hearts with his word. We hear over and over how our health is affected by the food we eat. What we feed our minds affects, not only our heath, but also our moods, our attitudes, our values, our relationships with others and with God. Questions we might ask ourselves are: 1) How much time do we spend reading trash? 2) How many hours a day is the TV on in our homes? 3) How much time do we sit at our Lord's feet letting him feed our minds and hearts with his presence? 4) How willing are we to believe him when he says: "heed me, and you shall eat well, you shall delight in rich fare. Come to me heedfully, listen, that you may have life." On average, I spend two hours a day in prayer. I'm not saying this to brag, but to assure you it is a real source of strength for me.

I would like to give an example of someone whose life changed and who was a dynamic force for good in the world because he let our Lord feed his mind and heart. The example is from the life of St. Ignatius Loyola who started the Jesuit order. He died in Rome on this day (July 31st) almost 450 years ago. In his younger years, St. Ignatius was a soldier, on his way to military fame and fortune. In a particular battle a cannon ball shattered his leg. During his long convalescence waiting for his leg to heal, he wanted to pass the time with some books about war and knights in shining armor, which were his favorite topics, but none were available. Gutenberg had lived only 100 years earlier, so there were not a lot of books to read. All Ignatius could find was a book about Christ and books on the lives of the saints. So out of desperation he read them. He tells us during this time something interesting happened to him. When he thought about worldly things and knights and fair damsels he felt intense pleasure. But when he gave these thoughts up out of weariness he felt dry and depressed. Yet when he thought of the saints and spiritual things he not only experienced pleasure but, even after he dismissed these thoughts, he still experienced great joy. He didn't notice this right away, but one day, in a moment of insight, it became obvious to him and he marveled at the difference.

St. Ignatius came to Christ and let himself be fed by Christ's Holy Spirit. It changed his life and it continues to influence the world for the better because of the spiritual renewal he began in the Church through his order. Life is full of stress and pressure for all of us. Sure we can see prayer and the Mass as one more thing to do, and it always feels that way before we start to pray or before we get ready to go to Mass, but when we truly open ourselves to its power we will receive a peace and strength that the world cannot give. Jesus promises it.

19th Sunday in Ordinary Time
August 10, 2008

INTRODUCTION – (1 Kings 19:9a, 11-13a, Romans 9:1-5, Matthew 14:22-33) Our first reading today takes us back roughly 860 years before Christ. The wicked Queen Jezebel was reigning in Israel at that time. The prophet Elijah was living in Israel at that time too. Jezebel was trying to lead God's people into paganism and Elijah was trying to keep them faithful to God. So there was conflict between them. She decided to have Elijah killed, and to save his life he had to get out of Israel. He fled to Mount Sinai. That was the place where God made a covenant with Israel and where he gave Moses the Ten Commandments four centuries earlier. When God spoke to Moses and the people who were fleeing Egypt, God spoke in thunder and lightening and earthquake. Elijah did not experience God in such powerful natural events but rather heard God in the silence of the desert.

HOMILY – The story of the Jews leaving Egypt and meeting God at Mt. Sinai tells us of a God who controls the forces of nature. They tell us of the fire and earthquake and thunder when God spoke to them on Mt. Sinai. Jesus too shows his power over the forces of nature when he walks on the water. Sometimes God communicates with us in a way that is powerful and unmistakable. It may not be in thunder and earthquake that God speaks to us. He may speak to us through a special healing or some prayer answered that we never thought possible. Those moments are worth treasuring. They are important to hold onto and remember when it seems God is quiet, for one of God's favorite ways of communicating with us is in silence. Like the prophet Elijah, we often need to discover God in the depth of our own hearts. And when we do find him there, we find him in dozens of other places too, which include the Scriptures and the Sacraments – especially the Eucharist.

In preparing my homily, I came across an interesting reflection on today's readings written by Fr. Grassi, a priest I met in Chicago a few years ago when I was there for a wedding. He said one of the most familiar nicknames for his city of Chicago is the "windy city." Most people think this name comes from the sometimes very strong winds that blow into the city from Lake Michigan. But, he said, Chicago was dubbed the "windy city" because of its history of long-winded politicians who would promise citizens everything and give them very little in actuality.

He applied this to the Church. Currently people have deep concerns about the church. There is no doubt there are some serious problems. Many people are self-appointed experts on just about every problem in the Church and every facet of church life. But sometimes all their talking can get in the way of living out the gospel of Jesus.

Perhaps the readings for today are telling us not to be so "windy." After all Elijah finds God not in the strong wind, but in a tiny whisper. The wind scares the apostles to the point where Peter almost drowns and needs Jesus to save him. Then Jesus calms the winds. Certainly there has to be communication, there has to be instruction and clarification. But there has to be silence too. Fr. Grassi concluded: maybe if we talked less and listened more it would be better for us and for the church. On that note I thought I would follow my own advice today and say: Amen.

Feast of the Assumption
August 15, 2008

INTRODUCTION ON THE FEAST – (Rev. 11, 19a; 12, 1-6a, 10ab; I Cor. 15, 20-27; Lk. 1, 39-56) The book of Revelation is highly symbolic. Some of the symbolism is quite obvious while it requires a fairly extensive knowledge of Scripture to interpret some of the other symbols. In today's first reading we hear about a woman, a child and a dragon. The dragon is the devil and the powers of evil at work in the world. The child is Christ. The woman in our reading has a double symbolism. She stands for Mary, the physical mother of Jesus Christ, and she stands for the Church, our spiritual mother who brings Jesus Christ to birth in us through faith and the sacraments. In today's passage the woman is rescued from the powers of the dragon and is described in great glory. This too has a double symbolism. It symbolizes the glory of Mary in the assumption. It also symbolizes God's faithful people whom he will rescue from evil and will bring, in the resurrection from the dead, into the glory of heaven.

HOMILY – Today's feast tells us that there is more to life than what we know and see right now. The feast is about Mary, but it's about us too, God's plan to raise us to new life to share with God eternal happiness. Mary gets to enjoy this privilege first after Jesus himself.

It is recorded nowhere in Scripture when, where or how Mary died. Nor do the Scriptures tell us about her assumption. It has been a part, however, of the very ancient tradition of the Church that Mary was assumed bodily into heavenly glory when her life here on earth was ended. One example comes from 450 in an early document where St. Juvenal, the Bishop of Jerusalem was asked by the emperor of Constantinople to bring the body of Mary to Constantinople. He replied to the emperor that Mary had died in the presence of all the apostles. But her tomb, when opened upon the request of St. Thomas, was found empty. Thus the apostles concluded that her body was taken up to heaven as Jesus was.

Some people belittle tradition as if it were unimportant. They claim to believe only the written words of the Scriptures. Yet, if we stop and think about it, we would have no Scriptures without tradition for the Scriptures came from the Church's tradition. For example, the earliest New Testament writings we have are the letters of Paul, the first of which was written about the year 51 A.D. Of our four gospels, Mark's is the first and it was written about 70 A.D. I say this so you can see the importance of tradition. The Church had only its tradition to go on until Paul and the evangelists started writing 20, 30, 40 years after Christ, at the earliest. So to say that the knowledge of the assumption of Mary came from the very early tradition of the Church is to give a lot of weight to this teaching. But to eliminate any question as to whether Mary actually was assumed into heavenly glory, the Holy Father, Pope Pius XII, after reviewing the belief of the Church through the ages, made it a dogma of our faith in 1950.

In today's gospel St. Luke tells us about Mary who is a young girl going to visit her much older cousin Elizabeth. Mary had just been visited by the angel, and she had accepted the invitation to be the mother of the Savior God was sending to his people. So she is at this moment unmarried and yet pregnant through the power of the Holy Spirit It was not a happy situation to be in. She could have been rejected by her husband to be, she could have been rejected by her family or could even have been put to death. Yet she is full of trust in God and praises God's greatness and God's goodness. There is no expression of "poor me." She is entirely focused on God. Mary shows us how to be trusting and in her assumption she shows us where that trust will lead us.

Today's feast honors Mary, for God himself has honored her. In her openness to God and in her willingness to always do whatever God wanted, God rewarded her in a unique way. But today's feast also is a source of hope for us. Christ came, as he tells us in St. John's gospel, that we might have the fullness of life. Our bodies too will share in that fullness as the Scriptures tell us so clearly. So Mary is allowed to enjoy ahead of time what God's plan is for all of us who are faithful in following him and serving him.

20th Sunday in Ordinary Time
August 17, 2008

INTRODUCTION – (Isaiah 56: 1,6-7, Romans 11: 13-15,29-32, Matthew 15: 21-28) The theme for today's liturgy is expressed in the psalm refrain: "O God, let all the nations praise you."

In order to prepare ourselves for today's first reading, I would like you to picture yourself as an observant Jew living in Jerusalem about 500 years before Christ. The temple was an important part of your faith and you could go there regularly for prayers and sacrifice. No one entered the temple except the priests when they made the daily offerings. The temple was God's house. Other men could pray in the area closest to the priests' court. The next area was the court for the women and, lastly, there was the court of the Gentiles. Those who were non-Jews were forbidden by death to go beyond the court of the Gentiles when approaching the temple. We heard Isaiah proclaim in today's first reading that foreigners (non-Jews) who kept the Sabbath and held to God's covenant would be welcome in the temple and could even offer sacrifices. God's house would be a house of prayer for all people and faith in God would be a saving grace for all people. That was as radical as a person could get at any time in Jewish history, especially 500 years before Christ.

It was even radical at the time of Jesus. When his followers started preaching the gospel to the Gentiles, they said the Gentiles, provided they followed Christ faithfully, were on equal footing with the Chosen People when it came to God's saving mercy and love.

In the second reading, from Paul's letter to the Romans, Paul laments the fact that the chosen people, by and large, have rejected Jesus as their Messiah and Savior. He sees great blessings coming upon the world if and when they ever do accept Christ.

HOMILY – O God, let all the nations praise you. Once a radical concept, but through the gospels it has been clearly shown that this is God's desire that all people be united in his love. What a wonderful world we would enjoy if this were to be.

Today's story about the Canaanite woman reflects both the fact that Jesus came to save all people and, at the same time, it reflects the tension that this idea created. Jesus did not respond when she made her request, and the apostles asked Jesus to get rid of her. She was becoming a nuisance. "Send her away," they said. It doesn't sound like the Jesus we usually hear about. Jesus' answer reflected the theology that the Jews were, after all, God's Chosen People, but he left her with an opening to argue her case further. In a demonstration of unwavering faith she responded with such cleverness and humility that Jesus could not refuse.

It's difficult to understand what was going on here. This is the only time in the gospels that Jesus turned away from anyone. He helped everyone, even pagans. Why was he resistant to helping this woman? First of all, Jesus was going into pagan territory, not so he could preach, but so that he and the apostles could get some rest. From St. Mark we learn that he didn't want anyone to know he was there. Secondly, he had previously told his apostles that their mission was to the lost sheep of the house of Israel, and when a person has a big job to do they have to stay focused. I feel there is more to the story, though, and this might be the piece of the puzzle I've been looking for. I came across an interesting study of the social and political dynamics of that region in the first century. Again we learn from what Mark tells us in his gospel that this woman would have been among the privileged, upper class, culturally Greek members of that region. She represented a class of people who were oppressing and exploiting poor Jewish farmers in Galilee at the time. It would not have been out of character for Jesus to reserve his ministry for the oppressed and to refuse the requests of those who exploited them. This may have been part of the story, but the gospels ignored that part because they were more interested in showing that Jesus could reach beyond the religious boundaries of the Jewish religion to bring salvation to those who were outside. Once more Mark's version is helpful for he quotes Jesus as saying, "let the children first be fed, for it is not fair to take the children's food and throw it to the dogs." This implies there would be a time when the other nations (the meaning of Gentiles) would be fed.

One last detail often bothers people in that Jesus refers to the Gentiles as "dogs." It sounds insulting and is unlike Jesus. Of course, Jesus was not one to avoid harsh criticism when it was warranted, but the Greek word here is not quite so harsh. It really means a little dog, a puppy or a pet, not a mangy cur that the word "dog" might make us think of. We're not even sure if the word was insulting in that culture. We ourselves use phrases that compare people with animals that are sometimes complimentary rather than insulting, such "he is a handsome dog," or "on the tennis court he's a tiger," or "she's a real chick."

One really valuable lesson we can take from hearing today's gospel is that Christ reaches out to all people in love, even those we don't think are worthy of his love. But there are a couple of other lessons we can take with us as well. Today's gospel is a good example of faith and perseverance in prayer. It also strikes me as a good example of asking others, including Jesus' good friends whom we call saints, to pray for us. Notice the woman tried to get the apostles to persuade Jesus for help and it worked. We don't understand the dynamics of prayer, but Jesus said there is great power in united prayer. And so we pray together the greatest prayer God gave us, the Eucharist. Amen.

21st Sunday in Ordinary Time
August 24, 2008

INTRODUCTION – (Isaiah 22: 19-23, Romans 11: 33-36, Matthew 16: 13-20) Shebna was a powerful man in the court of King Hezekiah in Judah, 700 years before Christ. Next to the king, he had the most powerful position in the kingdom. Shebna's power went to his head and he used his position to exploit the poor and the innocent in order to make himself exorbitantly rich. God said through Isaiah that Shebna needed to be replaced by a person with integrity. The only reason this passage was selected for today's reading was because of the reference to the key of the House of David. Keys are symbols of authority. In our gospel Jesus promises he would give Peter the keys to the kingdom of heaven.

HOMILY – I want to make a point about something I saw in the Enquirer this past week, then I want to reflect on two important ideas in today's gospel.

There was a brief news clip in Thursday's paper about a hacker who broke into the telephone system of FEMA last weekend and racked up about $12,000 in long distance phone calls to the Middle East and Asia. FEMA is part of Homeland Security. I didn't feel real secure after reading that! If this isn't a good incentive for people to pray for our country and our world, I don't know what is. Psalm 127 says: "If the Lord does not build the house, in vain do its builders labor; if the Lord does not watch over the city, in vain does the watchman keep vigil." We live in a society that keeps us so busy that often prayer is relegated to "something I'll do when I have the time." We are constantly being told our government is doing a great job of protecting us and I can only assume they are doing the best they can, but can we depend totally on the government? When was the last time we actually asked God to help our country. You might say a hacker breaking into a department of Homeland Security phone system and charging $12,000 in long distance phone calls is just a small thing, and maybe it is, but wars have been won and lost over seemingly small things. I say all this, not with the intent of frightening people, but with the intent of reminding all of us we need to constantly pray. "If the Lord does not watch over the city, in vain does the watchman keep vigil."

Now I want to reflect on two important ideas in today's gospel. First of all there are many places in the Scriptures that emphasize the preeminent position of Peter among the apostles, but there are two places where Peter's position of leadership is spelled out more clearly than anywhere else. The one is in St. John where Jesus tells Peter after the resurrection: "Feed my lambs, feed my sheep." Also in Scripture where Peter's position of importance is clearly emphasized is in today's gospel. Such insistence on the position of Peter vis-à-vis the other apostles is what underlies our belief that after Christ, the Holy Father is chief shepherd and head of the Church. His role is to be the visible representative of Christ. This doesn't mean he has perfectly represented Christ at all times in history, but that is still the position he holds. He has the final word on any issue relating to the Church. The keys Jesus said he would give Peter symbolize this authority. The keys Jesus gave Peter were not buried with him and that position of authority did not end when Peter died. It was passed on to his successors. This is implied in the gospel Matthew wrote, for Peter had been dead for at least 25 or 30 years when Matthew wrote this passage. Matthew made a big issue of this incident, not to tell us about some personal favor Jesus bestowed on Peter, but because the leadership position of Peter would remain as part of the structure of Christ's community of believers.

A second important idea in today's gospel is the answer to the question Jesus asked his apostles: "Who do you say that I am?" How we answer this question will determine how each of us relates to him. Is he, for example, someone worth our time on Sunday or even during the week? Is he someone we can trust? Is he someone who loves us, forgives us, wants only the best for us? Is he someone who has the authority to tell us how to live, what we should do, what we may not do? Is he someone we look forward to spending eternity with?

Can any of us give a complete and perfect answer to that question "Who do you say that I am?" In one way or another, each week I try to help you have a better sense of how to answer this question, even as I try to answer it for myself. It's easy to say Jesus is savior, Jesus is messiah, Jesus is Son of God, or as we say in the creed each week: Jesus is "God from God, light from light, true God from true God, etc." But has our mind and heart connected with these words to the extent that we can exclaim with Paul: "Oh, the depth of the riches and wisdom and knowledge of God! ... For from him and through him and for him are all things." The apostles could tell Jesus what others said about him, and we can also say what others have said about Jesus. That's okay, for that's how we begin to learn who Jesus is, by what others tell us. But have we moved beyond what others have told us to know Jesus in a personal way, a way that Jesus could say has not been revealed to us by "flesh and blood, but by the Heavenly Father?" If we do not know Jesus personally, what can we do that will help us to know him, not just by hearsay, but in a deeply personal way? How we do it is how we get to know anyone in a personal way. By spending time with a person. There are no shortcuts. Spending time with God, with Jesus, is called prayer. That's what we are about now. Amen.

22nd Sunday in Ordinary Time
August 31, 2008

INTRODUCTION – (Jeremiah 20, 7-9) Our first reading from the prophet Jeremiah goes back to 600 B.C. It sounds as if Jeremiah expected people would be grateful to him for speaking God's word to them. But they only hated him for it. The people ridiculed him, threw him in jail and even tried to kill him by throwing him in a well. We hear him complaining to God, "You duped me! You tricked me, God!"

Jesus' faithfulness to his mission would bring him suffering too, but Jesus did not feel tricked. He was well aware of what was going to happen. In today's gospel, we hear him warning his disciples ahead of time.

HOMILY – (Matthew 16, 21-27) You can't turn on the TV these days without hearing about politics. Will Rogers told a story you might enjoy that was about two politicians. One said to the other: "I'll stop telling lies about you, if you'll stop telling the truth about me."

Jesus would have made a lousy politician. Politicians are busy telling us how they are going to solve all our problems if we vote for them. Jesus is telling us if we follow him it's going to bring us problems. "Whoever wishes to come after me must take up his cross and follow me." Let us not assume from this statement that if we decide not to follow him, we'll be without any problems. Having problems comes with being human. Problems and crosses are part of everyone's life, whether they believe in Christ or not. Following Christ helps us deal with them more easily; the cross that we take up if we follow Christ will not defeat us but will bring us to resurrection.

Religion and philosophy have always tried to understand the mystery of suffering, especially the difficult problem of why good people suffer. So many ways to explain suffering are out there. None of them can take away all the mystery from suffering. For me, the best answer is found in the gospel. Jesus, through his cross and resurrection, has given us hope in our pain and hopelessness and has assured us that if we follow him in faith, that can only lead to eternal glory.

Peter had faith in Jesus as we heard in last week's gospel. He had just finished professing that Jesus was "the Messiah, the Son of the living God." The words were hardly out of his mouth when Jesus said that being faithful to his mission, that being the Messiah, would cost him his life, but he would rise again. That didn't match Peter's idea of the Messiah. In Peter's mind the Messiah would rally the Jewish people, he would defeat the Romans who occupied their land, he would bring back the days when Israel had their own king. That the Messiah would have to suffer was just not in the plan according to Peter. He was pretty bold telling Jesus "that's not going to happen to you. You're our savior. How can you save us by suffering? Ridiculous!" Jesus scolded Peter whom he had just praised for his faith and called him Satan. He was not saying Peter was evil. He was telling Peter he was doing Satan's job of being a tempter, trying to convince Jesus that being faithful to his mission would be a piece of cake. Jesus knew history better than Peter. He knew what the prophets before him went through – people like Jeremiah or Jesus' cousin John the Baptist, who was put to death by Herod. He could see things more clearly than Peter. Jesus told him "you have a lot to learn. You are thinking not as God does, but as human beings do."

We might wonder how Peter was expected to think like anything other than a human being. After all that's what he was. Peter wasn't the Son of God. But there was a way, and there is a way for us to think like God does; that is, to learn from God, to listen to him, to believe what he tells us. It's the way of prayer and faith. Basically that's no different than learning from any great teacher. When we learn from a great teacher, we absorb their thoughts, their insights, their perspective, their truth. We begin to think like them. When God tells us something and we listen and we believe it, we're seeing and knowing as God sees and knows, even if we can't fully understand everything at the time. We're beginning to think like God does. Peter's problem was he stopped listening to Jesus when Jesus started talking about suffering and he started to dictate to Jesus the way things were going to be. That's when he got into trouble.

We've been called to a life of prayer and faith. For us today, with freedom of religion, it is not as challenging for us to live that life as it was for those who followed Christ in the earliest days of the Church. People really did lose their lives and their fortunes for being Christians. We are blessed that we do not have to make the kind of life or death choice Christians did way back then. If we feel fortunate about it, shouldn't we be willing to share our faith with others? One good way to do that would be to invite them to come to church with you or to come to our RCIA program which begins this Wednesday.

Coming to Mass, as we are doing now, teaches us to think as God does. We listen to what God speaks to us in the Scriptures. We profess our faith in his word. As we struggle with our own crosses and difficulties, we celebrate how Jesus overcame his sufferings and his cross through the resurrection. In that event we are given a vision of God's plan of victory for all who live in his grace. Amen.

23rd Sunday in Ordinary Time
September 7, 2008

INTRODUCTION – (Ezekiel 33: 7-9, Romans 13: 8-10, Matthew 18: 15-20) Our first reading takes us back six hundred years before Christ as God explains to his prophet Ezekiel his responsibility as a prophet. Ezekiel must warn God's people of their sinful ways or he will be held accountable. It is a prelude to the gospel where Jesus instructs his followers how to help each other stay on the right track. St. Paul's teaching on love in our second reading reminds us that if we should try to correct one another it should be done out of love.

HOMILY – Each year, I always begin my introduction to our RCIA program with a lesson we can all learn from geese. I am borrowing these ideas from *Chicken Soup for the Soul (Vol 2)*. When we see geese flying south at this time of year, there is a reason why they fly that way. As each bird flaps its wings, it creates an uplift for the bird immediately following. This uplift that is provided by the V formation allows the flock to get to their destination more quickly and easily. They are traveling on the thrust of one another. It would seem logical that people who share a common direction can reach their destination more quickly and easily by traveling together and supporting one another. Apparently God thinks this is good idea too, so he gave us the Church. We can more quickly and easily reach our home with him if we travel together. We have an excellent guide in this journey and it is Jesus for he tells us in today's gospel: "Where two or three are gathered together in my name, there am I in the midst of them."

There's an attitude many have in society today that they don't need the Church. They can find God and love God on their own. Certainly we do have to come to know God in a personal way or our religion will simply be mechanical. But God in his wisdom gave us an important help to knowing him and serving him; that is, by being part of the Church, not just in name such as calling ourselves Christians, but by active participation in the Church.

There is another thing science knows about geese. When one of them falls out of formation, they quickly feel the drag and resistance of trying to go it alone and they get back into formation for the lifting power that is provided by the others. Unfortunately, when we humans try to go it alone spiritually, we are often slow to realize we are making no progress spiritually or we are even going in the wrong direction. If we have as much sense as a goose, we will stay connected with those people who are headed the same way we are. It's also interesting to note that if a bird gets sick or is injured, and falls out of formation, two others fall out with it and follow it down to give help and protection until it either gets well or dies. Then they will either launch out on their own or join a new formation until they can get back to their group. We have a responsibility to care for each other. St. Paul tells us today "owe nothing to anyone except to love one another for the one who loves another has fulfilled the law."

So, are you wondering why all this talk about Church? It's because our gospel today is about the Church. The word "church" (εκκλησία) is used over a hundred times in the Acts of the Apostles and in the Epistles of Paul. But our gospel today is only one of two places in all four of the gospels where the word is used. It is used once when Jesus tells Peter (the rock) that he would build his Church on him. Then it is used here where the issue of a serious sin that would be harmful to the Church needs to be dealt with. Jesus is saying an effort is to be made to win the sinner back to unity with the community. First a pastoral approach is to be taken. A one-on-one conversation between the offender and a friend or pastoral leader might do the trick. If not, an effort is to be made with the support of other members of the community to restore the sinner to good standing in the community. As a last resort, because the sinner refuses these efforts by the community, he or she is to be treated as one outside the community, with the hope this will shock them into being part of the community once again. We can read in 1 Corinthians how Paul had to do this with a person in the Church of Corinth who was living a publicly scandalous life and who rejected any efforts people made to get him to change his ways. All of this that Jesus talks about is to be done out of love for the sinner whom Christ wants to bring back to unity with God. It is done out of love for the Church, so others are not seriously harmed by someone leading them off in a wrong direction. Christ supports this action on the part of the Church by his statement, "whatever you bind on earth shall be bound in heaven."

Let me hasten to add this whole issue is not about a personal offense. Jesus deals with that a few verses later when Peter asks Jesus "if my brother sins against me, how often must I forgive him?" I'm sure we all remember the answer Jesus gave.

We differ from each other in many ways, yet we all have a common Father in heaven. We all have Christ as our savior who died to save us. We all wish to enjoy eternal life with God. The importance of working together, loving one another, supporting one another, praying for and with one another, cannot be overemphasized. As long as we follow Christ's lead and stay one with him and with each other in our journey, we will have all the help we need to get to where we want to go. We listen once again to Jesus' words in today's gospel: "where two or three are gathered together in my name, there am I in the midst of them." We trust in these words now as we continue to pray together the prayer he gave us at the Last Supper. Amen.

Feast of the Holy Cross
September 14, 2008

INTRODUCTION – (Numbers 21: 4b-9, Philippians 2: 6-11, John 3: 13-17) Our first reading takes us back over a thousand years before Christ, to the time when Moses was leading God's people from slavery in Egypt to the freedom of the Promised Land. The trip through the desert was extremely difficult and at times the people complained bitterly. One of their difficulties was an encounter with a nest of poisonous serpents whose bite brought intense suffering and burning pain and then death. The serpents were called saraph serpents, for saraph means "fiery." The people saw this as punishment for their complaining. But God gave them a way to be healed from the serpent's bite. The remedy might remind us of the symbol often used today as an icon of the medical profession. In today's gospel, Jesus compares this event to his crucifixion.

HOMILY – During Holy Week we focus on the sufferings of Christ crucified. Today our focus is more on the glory and victory of the cross. In Jesus' day the cross was an instrument of torture, brutality and shame. The Romans reserved it for the worse criminals and enemies of the Roman Empire. If a criminal was a Roman citizen, he or she was exempt from crucifixion because it was such a terrible way to die. Roman citizens were simply beheaded. But Jesus has turned the cross into a symbol of victory, a symbol of hope, a symbol of sacrifice and infinite love. St. Paul tells us in Galatians (2,20) "I live by faith in the Son of God who has loved me and given himself up for me."

Over and over the Scriptures tell us through the cross Jesus saved us, but early Christian art seldom pictured the cross. They didn't need to. Father Foley in *Saint of the Day* said: "It stood outside too many city walls, decorated only with decaying corpses, as a threat to anyone who defied Rome's authority." Included in this group of those who defied Rome's authority were the Christians who would not worship pagan gods, but only the Father, the Lord Jesus and the Spirit. The emperor Constantine who made Christianity legal in 313 also eliminated crucifixion as a form of capital punishment. Once the Roman Empire actually ceased crucifying people, then images of the cross appeared in Christian art. These first images of the cross did not include an image of the suffering Christ, but they were crosses decorated with jewels and precious metals. Incidentally it was a vision of the cross that led to the conversion of Constantine. He was assured in the vision that in the sign of the cross he would conquer Maxentius, a rival to the throne, and he would become emperor of Rome.

Once Constantine gained control of the Roman Empire, he went to the Holy Land with his mother, St. Helen, to discover the places where Jesus lived and died. Constantine and his mother had churches built in Bethlehem and the Mount of Olives but the most famous church he built is the Church of the Holy Sepulcher, built over the hill of Calvary and the tomb of Jesus. It was in the process of building the Church of the Holy Sepulcher that Jesus' cross was found. How did they know it was Jesus' cross? Legend has it that the men working on this project found three crosses and they didn't know which one was Jesus' cross. They touched each of the crosses to a woman who was dying and when she was touched with the third cross, she was instantly healed. Today's feast of the Holy Cross goes back to that time, around the year 320 AD. It celebrates the finding of the true cross and the dedication of the Basilica of the Holy Sepulcher. So that's why this feast is celebrated in the middle of September and not during Lent as we might expect.

Today's gospel is sometimes called the gospel in miniature. These few verses express the essence of the entire gospel: God's offer of eternal life through the sacrifice of Christ, a sacrifice offered out of love for us. God so loved the world, God so loved you and me that he gave us the greatest gift, the gift of his son, so we would know the greatest blessing: eternal happiness with him.

Today we approach the cross not with sorrow but with joy, not as a symbol of death but of life, not as a sign of defeat but of victory, not as a cause for fear but of hope, not as an instrument of cruelty and hatred but of eternal love. On a practical level, I know somehow it was inevitable if Jesus were to be true to his mission. If he had run away from it, he would not have risen and his message would have soon been forgotten. Today Christians make up one third of the world's population. If Jesus had abandoned his mission to change the world through love, perhaps some obscure history book might have had a sentence or two about this person who did a lot of healing and was a good preacher, but for the most part his ministry would be forgotten. This is just a superficial explanation of the mystery of the cross. There is much more to this mystery, but each of us has to discover it for ourselves. To come to a deeper understanding takes lots of prayer – and that's what the Mass does for us each week, it reminds us of God's love and the hope and joy and freedom and peace and salvation it gives us. Amen.

24th Sunday in Ordinary Time
September 15, 2008

HOMILY – (Sirach 27:30–28:7, Romans 14:7-9, Matthew 18:21-35) Jesus is talking about one of his favorite topics, forgiveness. As a counselor I know what unforgiveness does to the individual who cannot let go of pain or hurt someone has caused them. And as a ordinary citizen, just reading the paper tells me what unforgiveness does to nations, as they keep trying to get even with one another for some real or imagined act of cruelty. Some of the battles between different nationalities have roots that go back hundreds of years. Jesus is telling us we have to go even beyond the moderate rule of "eye for an eye and a tooth for a tooth." I couldn't find the exact quote, but I think it was Martin Luther King who said, if we all insisted on an eye for an eye and a tooth for a tooth, soon everyone in the world would be blind and toothless. We can't hold on to our hating and desire for revenge forever.

Besides having today's readings remind us about the importance of forgiveness, today is also Stewardship Sunday. That means I get to talk about one of my favorite topics: money. Actually, it's not one of my favorite topics. Fortunately the people of St. Boniface have been very supportive of their parish and I have to talk about it only infrequently. But once in a while I do have to deal with "money," especially on Stewardship Sunday.

You know "the love of money is the root of all evil," St. James tells us. Money can buy a house, but not a home. It can buy a bed, but not sleep. It can buy a clock, but not time. It can buy you a book, but not knowledge. It can buy you a position, but not respect. It can buy you medicine, but not health. It can buy you blood, but not life. It can buy you sex, but not love. How many times have we heard it said: "money isn't everything." And it often causes pain and suffering. I tell you all this because I care about all of you. As your friend, I want to help you reduce pain and suffering in your life. So send me all your money and I will suffer for you!

Like that? It was a good story for Stewardship Sunday. Today's parable is another good story. You know, a good story has many applications, and today's gospel is an excellent illustration of stewardship. A couple of things might help us get a feel for this story. Our translation tells us the man owed a huge amount. The original version (in the Greek) says the man owed his king ten thousand talents. In today's money that would be about 2 or 3 billion dollars. It was customary for people who couldn't pay off their debts to be sold into slavery. That was the way society worked. The king's generosity was beyond belief. The man whose debt was cancelled was owed (again looking at the original Greek) a hundred denarii. Translated into today's dollars, that's about $5000. It boggles our mind to think that anyone could be as selfish as the man in today's gospel. He is an tremendous example of what stewardship is not. He was given so much and in spite of the unbelievable example of generosity shown by his king, he hadn't learned how to be generous with anything.

Stewardship means we recognize what we have been given isn't just for our own selfish use. We're not in this world only for our own benefit, but we're here to help one another. And what we have, we're not going to take with us. The only thing we will take with us is our love for God and our love for others. Developing an attitude of stewardship, teaches us how to love. It also teaches us how to be grateful. What haven't we been given? Even the things we have acquired by our own industry we owe in gratefulness to our creator, for God gave us the time and talent and positive stimuli that influenced our lives to make it possible for us to accomplish what we have. Stewardship is awareness of how indebted we are to God and to others. It is gratitude. It is love. It is sharing. There are lots of needs in our world today. A lot of people here I am sure have real needs in their own families, so I'm not trying to take all your money as my humorous little comments suggested. I'm not even trying to take all of your charitable donations for St. Boniface. But I do have to speak up for our parish every now and then, or I would not be a good steward, a good caretaker of this parish.

Last year you might remember, we ran short for the year, and I asked people if they could to increase their donations by about 10%. Many $10 donations went up to $11 and many $20 donations went up to $22. I thank you. It worked. This year, on June 30, we ended our fiscal year ahead by $5,470. That's good. And I bet most of those who increased their donations by a dollar or two didn't miss that extra few dollars at the end of the month.

Our big expense this year will be a new boiler for the church and the school. The estimate came in for $41,600. With asbestos removal the cost will be over $50,000. We have one boiler, but it won't carry the load all by itself. We do have a couple of cheaper options, but they could cost us more $$$ in the future. This was the best choice. Normally I might have to have a special appeal for the funds, but we were blessed this year. Recently, a person in this neighborhood left us a bequest of $30,000 in his will. This is a good thing to keep in mind when you make out your will. Remember your parish. You've never seen a Brinks truck following a hearse! All we'll take with us is our love for God and the good deeds we have done for others. With this bequest, I'm hoping if people can be just a little bit more generous, we won't have to have a special appeal. Another topic: People have asked what's going on with the bells. We have a figure from Verdin, the company that put them in, in the first place, for about $30,000. We're still trying to see if we can fix them cheaper. The first thing we need to do is clean out the bell tower. The pigeons have been using it for a bathroom and burial ground, so we have to start there before we can do anything else. Stay tuned on this one.

I could spend a long time telling you about stained glass windows, roofs, boilers and bells. But I think what I've said will give you a good enough picture of where we are financially. Whatever you can do to help out will be greatly appreciated. The parish has always come through in the past, so I'm confident we'll do OK and I want to say a big "thank you" to those who keep St. Boniface going, not only with donations of treasure, but also with donations of time and talent. Amen.

25th Sunday in Ordinary Time
September 21, 2008

INTRODUCTION – (Isaiah 55: 6-9; Philippians 1: 20c-24,27a, Matthew 20: 1-16) When God's people were in exile in Babylon, they were as depressed as anyone could possibly be. They had lost everything. They were sure they had even lost God's love because of their sinfulness. Today we hear God's prophet assure them it is never too late to return to the Lord. Even though they knew they were not worthy of it, they will have God's mercy if they will reform their lives. God is forgiving, not because we are worthy, but because it is God's nature to be generous and forgiving. The theme of God's generosity prepares us for today's gospel.

HOMILY – Jesus' parables, as always, are designed to shock us into thinking. It's normal for us to feel the employer was unfair and that's exactly how Jesus knew we would feel. It is true, the owner was more generous with some than with others, but was he unfair with anyone?

In Jesus' society a laborer was paid at the end of the day and the normal pay was just enough for a person to feed his family for one day. Could it be that the owner of the vineyard was more generous with some so that none of the people who worked for him that day would have to beg, borrow or steal in order to feed their families the next day? Would that be unfair for the employer to do that? What do you think Jesus was trying to tell us?

The clue to understanding the parable is the first line where Jesus tells us this is what the kingdom of heaven is like. Jesus was telling us why he was always willing to reach out to sinners, something he was frequently criticized for doing. He wants us to know it's never too late to find God if we wish to. Remember the good thief whom Jesus forgave on the cross. If we've not been living right, though, does that mean we can wait until the last minute to straighten ourselves out? If we do we'll miss out on the joy of knowing God's love and presence in our lives right now and who knows whether we'll get the opportunity to repent at the last minute. I think it was St. Augustine who prayed: "God, make me good, but not right now!" Not a good prayer. Fortunately God paid attention only to the first part of the prayer (God, make me good), and the Church was greatly blessed because God led Augustine from his wayward life to a life of holiness. "The usual daily wage" in the parable is a symbol for the immense happiness we will all have in God's kingdom. Some individuals may be closer to God because they served and loved God more faithfully than others, but we will all be equal in one way, whether we receive God's grace early or late in life, we will all be as happy as we can possibly be.

Jesus explained his forgiveness of sinners by this parable. St. Matthew found it helpful to use this same parable for a similar purpose when he wrote his gospel probably 50 or 60 years after Jesus preached it. During this period, many Jewish Christians, who had lived their whole lives faithful to God's law, had difficulty accepting new converts into the Church, converts coming from paganism, who represented those who came late to the vineyard. The parable was meant to help Jewish Christians welcome those who came to know Christ later in life and accept them as equals in God's kingdom.

Today we have no problem with these ideas. We are always happy to see people turn their lives toward God, whether they had strayed away at some time in their lives and came back, or whether for the first time, even late in life, they become believers in Christ and join his

Church. But there may be a couple of ideas that are relevant for us today. First of all, the people who worked all day complained about unfair treatment. Is Jesus telling us we shouldn't complain when we feel we've been treated unfairly? Well, sometimes complaining is good. It sometimes helps get things done, it helps us get things off our chest, it may help us clarify our thoughts and come to realize we haven't been treated too badly after all. If people didn't complain, counselors and psychologists and doctors would not be able to help people. Politicians wouldn't have anything to do. Friends and family members wouldn't be able to give support and sympathy to each other if they didn't know how their friend or family member hurt. Complaining can be positive, but we have to be careful not to make it a way of life. If we want to complain, it helps to stop and count our blessings and we might realize God has treated us far better than any of us deserve!

The other idea today's parable connects with is envy. Envy makes us miserable. Envy is when we look around at others and think they have much more than we do, they have had more breaks in life than we have, etc. We feel life is not fair and we are depressed over it. I believe God is more than fair with all of us. If we want to compare ourselves with others, we need to compare ourselves also with those who have not been as blessed as we have. Always wanting more may motivate us to achieve in life, but it can also be a formula for constant unhappiness. We need to always focus on the positive, on our blessings and give thanks. I always preach that the key to joy in life is gratitude. God's ways are not our ways, Isaiah tells us. Part of the joy of eternity will be praising God for his abundant love and goodness to us. The "Eucharist" which we pray now, a word which means "thanksgiving," is the most perfect way to do that. Amen.

26th Sunday in Ordinary Time
September 28, 2008

INTRODUCTION – (Ezekiel 18: 25-28, Philippians 2:1-11, Matthew 21: 28-32) In 587 B.C. when the Babylonians conquered the Jews, destroyed their cities and their Temple, and made the Jews who were still alive after the conquest into their slaves, the Jews concluded they were being punished for the sins of previous generations. They complained that God was not fair. In today's first reading from Ezekiel, God addresses the Jews in exile instructing them that their own refusal to hear God's prophets and to follow God's laws led them to the disaster they were suffering. But, God says, the situation was not hopeless. They could always turn back to God if they wanted. This reading prepares us for the gospel where we hear a similar message. If we have damaged our relationship with God, we can always turn back.

HOMILY – Jesus asks for our thoughts about the story we just heard in St. Matthew's gospel. "What do you think of this? A man had two sons." I do not want to confuse things, but I wonder if you remember another parable that begins: "A man had two sons." This other parable is in St. Luke and if you do not know which one it is, it is the story of the prodigal son. The older son was an obedient and hard working son. The younger decided he wanted his share of the inheritance so he could get off the farm and go have lots of fun in the big city. After he spent all his inheritance, he realized what a fool he had made of himself and came home to a most loving and forgiving father. Today's gospel from Matthew is somewhat similar. There are two sons. In Matthew's story the father had a problem with both of his sons. However, the son who said "no" to his father realized he made a mistake and changed his mind. That is key to understanding both parables. The prodigal son and the son who told his father "I will not" in today's gospel both had a change of heart. The son in today's parable who said "no" to his father wasn't as bad as the son who blew away half his father's money. It may not sound like a big deal in today's culture – a lot of kids have no trouble saying "no." But when I was growing up, it was close to committing suicide to say "I will not" to my father. After his change of heart, the son was soon working side by side with his father in the vineyard and was back in his father's good graces.

Jesus' point, in both of these parables as in everything he taught us, is it's never too late to change our mind if we have not been living the way God wants us to. Ezekiel had the same message in today's first reading. He told the Jews in exile to take responsibility for what they did and stop making excuses or blaming someone else.

We live in a world where anything we've ever done can come back to haunt us. If we were a goof off in school, if we got in trouble with the law, smoked pot, got a traffic ticket, had to declare bankruptcy, robbed a bank or whatever, it's all there in someone's memory and perhaps in public records. Especially if we tried to run for public office. The media would let the world know everything we did, and everything anyone related to us did as well. To some extent that makes sense. What a person did in the past tells a lot about their character and may be a predictor or what they'll do in the future. It's the only basis on which we can evaluate someone, to decide whether we want them as our president, or our friend or our doctor or financial advisor or someone we can trust with our children. But God judges us differently and that's because he can see what kind of person we are right now. If we've been bad and decide to change, he sees our change of heart. Conversely, if we've been good and decide otherwise, he sees that too. Today's gospel tells us no matter what we've done in the past, it's where we are now that matters with God. It's a message that brings healing and peace if we've made mistakes in the past (and who hasn't because we're all sinners). I have a little story to tell that I love. I got it from Scott Peck. There was a lady who claimed that Jesus was appearing to her. And she went to tell her bishop about it. He was skeptical and said he wanted some proof it was happening. So he told her that the next time Jesus appeared to her she was to ask Jesus what the bishop confessed the last time he went to confession. The next time she saw the bishop he asked her to report on what happened. Did she ask Jesus what the bishop said the last time he went to confession? She did ask she said. "And what did he answer?" the bishop asked. She said he forgot. Scott Peck said that was a genuine vision or the lady was a pretty smart cookie because that's the way it is with God: when we repent and change our hearts, God forgets the past. It brings healing and peace to know that we can change and God gives us a chance to start over. The message in today's gospel should also shake a few people out of their spiritual lethargy if they, like the son who didn't show up at work, say to themselves it doesn't matter how I live or what I do, God won't notice. Yes God will.

As I conclude, let us return to another lesson from the parable of the prodigal son. There were two sons. Remember the older son was very responsible. He worked hard on the farm. He never did anything to displease his father, but he resented his father for welcoming his younger brother back and celebrating when he returned. The older son lacked compassion. God wants us to be responsible, hard working, obedient and faithful and we will be blessed. He wants us to say "yes" and be willing to follow him when he calls, that is the point of today's gospel. He wants us to have a compassionate heart as well: "have in you the same attitude that is also in Christ Jesus," St. Paul tells us in today's second reading. When Jesus asks in today's gospel: "What is your opinion?" he is asking what kind of son or daughter are you and am I. Are we like any of these sons we heard about today. Or are we like Christ, the faithful Son who always says "yes" to the Father and goes to work doing what he asks of us. If we're lots of talk and offer lots of excuses and blame others for why we don't do what God wants, God can see right through us and it will get us nowhere. If we've said "no" to the Father, we can change our mind. If we feel we've been pretty faithful to God throughout our lives, trying to always say "yes" and doing what God wants, then there are a few things we need to pray for: pray to be humble, thank him for the graces he's given us, pray for the grace to remain close to him, pray for those who have forgotten about God and ask for a heart that does not hold grudges. Amen.

27th Sunday in Ordinary Time
October 5, 2008

INTRODUCTION – (Isaiah 5:1-7; Philippians 4: 6-9, Matthew 21:33-43) Most of us know how much work is involved in caring for a garden. Just imagine how much work is involved with setting up an entire vineyard, which is a full time business. Isaiah describes some of what was involved in today's first reading. If we wonder why there needed to be a watchtower in the vineyard, it was needed, both day and night, to protect the grapes from thieves and predators, especially during harvest time. Apparently Isaiah was a musician as well as a talented poet. As he sang his song we can imagine the shock his audience felt when they discovered they were the vineyard he was singing about. From history we know Isaiah's prophecy literally came to be true when the Assyrian invasion came and much of the land was laid waste.

HOMILY – As I reflected on today's readings about vineyards, I thought back about 40 years to a day when I was traveling with my sister, brother, and sister-in-law in Germany. My brother and I had a great love for Mosel wine at that time and we spent the whole day driving down along the Mosel river, just looking at vineyards. At the end of the day we stopped in a little place to get something to eat. We were tired and thirsty and ordered some of the local wine. It was cold and delicious and, since we hadn't had much to eat or drink that day, it hit us hard. We both started laughing at the silliest things. My sister (a nun) was much irritated at the two of us, which made us laugh all the more. I guess I wasn't very sensitive to my sister at the time, but my brother and I sure had a fun time.

At the time I just enjoyed the benefits of all those vineyards and hardly thought of all the work involved in making it possible for us to enjoy ourselves. Maintaining a vineyard is a year round operation, caring for the vines, pruning them for the best yield, protecting them from anything or anyone who might destroy them, pressing the grapes, storing the juice until it ferments, etc., etc. Vineyards were abundant in Judea at the time of Jesus, so it's natural Jesus would base his story on something his listeners were very familiar with. Jews used lots of wine, in liturgies and at meals, yet they always respected it. Jews have one of the lowest rates of alcoholism among all nationalities. Today we have two stories about vineyards.

In the first story from Isaiah, over 700 years before Christ, the vineyard represented the people of Israel who were a great disappointment to God. God made them his own special people and blessed them abundantly; yet they turned their back on him and the commandments he had given them. Their lives represented sour grapes after all God had done for them.

In the second story from the gospel, the vineyard represents God's people, but it is the religious leaders of Jesus' time who are taken to task. They ignored their responsibilities to God and controlled and led God's people, not in God's ways, but to protect their own interests. We can see the first set of servants who were sent to the tenant farmers as representing the earlier prophets like Amos, Hosea, Isaiah and the second group of servants representing the later prophets like Jeremiah and Ezekiel and others. The son who was put to death was Jesus, of course. I wonder if the parable would apply to the leaders of our modern culture who tell us God is like some big jolly Santa Claus who's going to give to every person everything they want to be happy when they die. This is the popular theology – everyone is going to heaven no matter how they lived. Whether they prayed and went to church or not, whether they hurt or cheated others; none of that matters. But that's not what Jesus taught us. The ten commandments are still in force.

Today is Pro-Life Sunday. One of the worst sins of our culture is abortion, the killing of an innocent, defenseless human life. People rationalize all over the place about this issue, but it is a fact that innocent human life is deliberately being destroyed, mostly so as not to embarrass or inconvenience the person who is carrying that life. People who were not planning to conceive often are looking for help to know what to do.

Pro-life programs offer that help. Special envelopes are in the pews today to offer support to pro-life programs and organizations. There is an article in today's bulletin that challenges us to realize that abortion is not the only way our culture does not support life and how we can become in all ways more the kind of person God calls us to be in today's second reading: true, honorable, pure, just and gracious in whatever we do. Amen.

28th Sunday Ordinary Time
October 12, 2008

INTRODUCTION – (Isaiah 25:6-10a; Philippians 4:12-14, 19-20, Matthew 22:1-14) Today's first reading and today's gospel give us a beautiful picture of what it is we're praying for when we say "thy will be done." God's will is for our complete and eternal happiness. Our gospel warns us, however, that in order to be part of his beautiful plan, we need to respond to the invitation he offers us.

Our second reading is part of a thank you note St. Paul wrote to the Philippians for the money they sent him to help him most probably while he was in prison. The Philippian community was the only community that were thoughtful enough to offer him any support in his ministry. Responding to the invitation God gave him to serve as an apostle was a difficult job for Paul.

HOMILY – Heaven is going to surpass all our hopes and expectations. It's going to be more wonderful than we can imagine. Because there will be love and joy and peace like we've never experienced, it's hard for God to tell us about it. All he can do is to use images that we are familiar with: a great banquet, a wedding feast, the elimination of suffering and death, wealth that cannot be exhausted as in the hidden treasure, the pearl of great price or the mansion God is preparing for us. Today we heard Isaiah compare it to a great banquet and Jesus compare it to a wedding celebration for a prince which would be an event people would remember for years.

As Jesus tells us, to have all this wonder and joy we must respond to an invitation. We must be wise enough not to turn it down. How will we recognize the invitation when it comes? As I reflected on this week's gospel, I came up with a long list of ways we might recognize it. I won't bore you with everything on my list but just give you a few ideas of how we might recognize it. It sounds something like this: "Come to me all you who labor and are burdened and I will refresh you." Or "I am the good shepherd," a shepherd whose sheep hear his voice and follow him. We hear the invitation in the sermon on the mount when Jesus tells us: "Everyone who listens to these words of mine and acts on them will be like a wise man who built his house on rock." Or from the Book of Revelation: "Behold I stand at the door and knock. If anyone hears my voice and opens the door, then I will enter his house and dine with him and he with me." He doesn't promise everything will be wonderful in this world if we respond to his call, for: "If anyone would come after me, let him take up his cross and follow me." But for those who do respond, he promises "I will be with you always." "I will not leave you orphans." In a special way he invites us to begin enjoying the wonderful banquet heaven will provide when he tells us, "Unless you eat the flesh of the son of man and drink his blood you do not have life in you." He invites us each morning to "take this and eat, take this and drink." For Catholics this is part of his invitation to "Keep holy the Lord's day."

You might say that's a commandment, not an

invitation. Yes, he does command us because we don't always feel like doing what we should, but today he invites us for he wants us to come to him not just because we're commanded, but he wants us to come because we want to, he wants us to come out of love.

There is one part of the parable that puzzle many people and that is the last part about the wedding garment. Some scholars have suggested that wedding garments were provided to guests as they arrived because the king, apparently a kind and generous man, would not have responded with such anger if they were not extremely important and easily obtainable. Jesus uses this part of the parable to warn his followers that even though a person says they believe in him, it's not going to help them much if they do not put their faith into action.

Our new age theology wants us to think that everyone is going to be blessed in the next life. Jesus is telling us eternal happiness is not to be taken for granted. The way to eternal happiness is open for all, but we have a free will as to how we will respond. May the banquet we come to today, eating his body and drinking his blood, lead us to the eternal banquet he has prepared for us. Amen.

29th Sunday in Ordinary Time
October 17, 1999

INTRODUCTION – (Isaiah 45:1, 4-6, 1 Thessalonians 1:1-5b, Matthew 22:15-21) A person of faith can see God at work even in what appears to be purely secular events. Five hundred and eighty seven years before Christ, the Jews had been conquered by the Babylonians and had been taken to Babylonia as captives and slaves. Fifty years later, the Persians conquered the Babylonians and the king of Persia, Cyrus, decided to let the Jews return home. Not only did he permit them to return to rebuild their homes and cities, but being a very tolerant person, he encouraged them to rebuild their temple to their God, Yahweh. The prophet Isaiah, in today's first reading, refers to this pagan ruler as God's anointed and through the prophet, God tells his people that it was God who gave Cyrus his victories and who led Cyrus to liberate the Jews. This reading connects with the gospel in that Jesus gave deference to the Romans who occupied Israel at that time, but he also reminds us that God's position cannot be usurped.

HOMILY – No one loves paying taxes. But the Jews at the time of Jesus especially hated taxes, because most of the taxes went to Rome, the government that controlled Israel. They were in a situation similar to the one we were in 250 years ago when America was an English colony. England controlled our government, took our taxes and sent its troops to patrol our cities. We fought to gain our independence and we did. The Jews fought too at times, but were always defeated. The Jews bitterly resented taxes, not only because Rome took most of them, but because the money was too often spent extravagantly, there was lots of corruption among government officials, the collection of taxes was heartless and the country was impoverished. Whenever I think of the situation they were in, I picture an olive press I visited in Israel that was in operation at the time of Jesus. It was built into a hillside. There was a fake wall in the room where the olives were pressed and behind it was a hidden storage area where they could hide some of their oil from the tax appraiser. But then again, I guess that's nothing unusual. People still try to hide their income today too. The Jews were trying to set Jesus up in asking him this question about taxes. We can see the setup especially in the two groups that approached him: the Pharisees and the Herodians. These two groups were not the least bit friendly toward one another. The Pharisees prided themselves as most strict observers of the Jewish law, and Jewish law would dictate that God alone was ruler and Lord of Israel and not Caesar. So they would have seen taxes a blasphemy. The Herodians are believed to have been a party that supported the rule of Rome and of Herod, their local king. This question that was asked of Jesus was indeed a hot issue. If Jesus approved paying the taxes he would have stirred up the people's anger, because the people bitterly resented the taxes. And if he said don't pay the taxes this could have led to his arrest as a revolutionary. Jesus answer caused the people to marvel. The challenge of his answer, of course is knowing just what things are Caesar's and what things are God's.

What I think Jesus does enunciate here is the important principle of keeping things in balance. We have many needs in life. We have to take care of ourselves physically, we need time for work, for fun, for family, for friends, for learning, for our spiritual needs. It's so easy to let one area of our lives get out of control at the expense of another area. And this can cause many problems. The most obvious example is in the area of addiction: whether it is work addiction, or alcohol or sex or gambling or food or drugs or whatever. In less dramatic ways harm can be done by spending too much time pursuing entertainment or sports or keeping up with the Jones's. Even in the area of food, it is important to eat a balanced diet, eating beans and grains and vegetables and fruit and not just meat and potatoes or sweets.

Scott Peck in the book *The Road Less Traveled* said the key to balance is "giving up." "Giving up" the pleasure, the thrill, the high, the excitement that some things can give us in order to attend to areas of our lives that are also important, but maybe not so physically or emotionally stimulating. This takes a certain amount of self-discipline and possibly even outside help if a person is dealing with an addiction. Much of my earlier life as a priest I was always getting sick and it took me a while to realize that I was trying to do more than I was able. I had to realize my physical limitations. I had to "give up" the joy that comes from helping people and the high that achievement can give in order to make sure I got enough rest. A psychiatrist once said, one of the hardest things for a man to realize is that he is not God. We have to be realistic about our limitations and live within them. In a similar way, some people do not realize their financial limits and they spend themselves into great debt. That's also a form of getting things out of balance.

One of the areas of our lives that many people tend to neglect is the spiritual. That's why we're here today, to remember there is more to life than getting up in the morning, going to work, going to bed at night and starting over the next day. We are here to care for the spiritual part of ourselves. That's what Jesus is talking about in the gospel. Giving to God what belongs to God may not have the excitement of a basketball game, or the pleasure of staying in bed on a Sunday morning. Yet, we are told in the third commandment to "keep holy the Lord's day." We've pretty much reduced his day to one hour and for some people even that's too much to ask. It's not all God said we owe him. We could talk about charitable giving as in the mission collection for next week. Ultimately, we owe God for everything we have. "What do we have that we have not received?", St. Paul asks us. Catholics as a group make more money than most other denominations yet in terms of percent of giving we are among the stingiest. I'm not trying to sneak in another money talk here. I'm just pointing out God asks for more than time from us. And why? Not for his good, but for our own. We all have a spiritual part to ourselves and that part of us needs to be nurtured too. And although we need other things like rest, food, family, friends, and fun, the spiritual part of us is the only part that will survive. The only thing we will take with us when we leave this world are the things we have done to serve God and the good works we have done for others, nothing else. Our eternal happiness will depend on that. That should certainly be enough motivation to "give up" something that will benefit us momentarily in this life in order to make room for something that will benefit us forever. It takes mainly self-discipline to do this, and faith. Let me conclude by thanking you for your faith and your prayer as you offer the gift of your time and yourself to our Lord on this "the Lord's day."

30th Sunday in Ordinary Time
October 26, 2008

HOMILY – (Exodus 22: 20-26, 1 Thessalonians 1: 5c-10, Matthew 22: 34-40) We have a short gospel today, but the ideas it contains are enormous. Numerous volumes have been written about each of these themes, love for God and love for others. Often when I prepare a couple for marriage, I ask them what they think love is. Answers range from a very well thought out response involving the notion of self-giving to a smirky, embarrassed answer like "well, you know." TV and movies seem to portray only one kind of love, the kind of love that could be described as a wonderfully pleasant, euphoric kind of feeling that seems to promise fulfillment and happiness forever but its underlying function is to facilitate mating. Its promise of fulfillment and happiness forever is generally misleading and temporary. This kind of love has a lot to recommend it: 1) if it didn't exist probably very few of us would have been conceived, 2) it is a taste of the joys of heaven, and 3) it sells movies, books, magazines and TV programs and that's why we hear a lot about it. I have seen many marriages fail because one or the other person believes this is the only kind of love there is or the only kind of love that really matters. When the romantic "high" dims, they move on. But those who realize there is a lot more to love than romance work through challenging times in relationships. They discover a depth of love that may be lacking in fireworks but is more secure and more deeply joyful. Fortunately our faith keeps reminding us there are many facets and stages of love and not just one kind.

Our English language, with its vast vocabulary, uses only one word, love, for a multitude of emotions, attitudes, expressions and activities. Even the Greeks 2000 years ago had three different words for love: eros – passionate love (hence the word erotic), philia – friendship love (hence the name Philadelphia: the city of brotherly love) and agape – love that is compassionate, generous, faithful, unselfish and able to reach out even to our enemies.

Several years ago I used some ideas from Dr. M. Scott Peck, a psychiatrist and ordained Episcopal priest. I would like to repeat some of his thoughts because they are so illustrative. He tells us we often confuse love with affection and there are significant differences between the two. He tells us "affection is mostly an emotion between equals... On the other hand, we can love virtually anyone if we set our minds to it. Liking or affection is primarily a feeling; love is primarily a matter of decision and action." This may sound abstract, but it has practical applications. For example, when working with some of his patients, he helped them to understand they were not obliged to like all of their relatives and this paradoxically made it easier for them to love them.

I think Dr. Peck gave a lovely example from his own marriage of how love grows and matures. I found this very insightful. He and his wife, Lily, were married for 40 years. He said as the bloom of their romantic love faded, there was at first denial. They worked hard to act like it couldn't be happening. When that didn't work and they were faced with their profound differences (which, of course, they perceived as faults in each other) they became angry at each other and even angrier as they attempted, without success, to somehow change the other. When that failed, they eventually descended into a lengthy phase of depression wherein each wondered whether it was worth it all. He then says gradually, mysteriously and almost miraculously, they emerged into a stage where increasingly they began to accept their deep differences of personality as mere differences, often more reflective of virtue than fault. Their marriage had come to a point where he described Lily as his best friend with whom he could have lots of fun and enjoy many common interests. I thought their story was a good example how love can develop and grow.

I see this same pattern take place in people's relationship with God. There are moments in our spiritual lives when we discover God's love and presence and it is powerful and wonderful. Those "high" moments may come early in our relationship or they may come after years of praying and serving God. When they come it brings a "high" we never want to let go of. In the normal course of any relationship, even our relationship with God, there are periods when we feel as if we are in a desert. There are times when we get angry with God, when we try to make deals, when we feel let down because he doesn't give us what we want. If we weather all these stages and do not give up faith, all these stages will lead to a deep love and a profound joy.

I could talk on love for a long time, because as I said earlier, much has been written about it. But I wish to briefly conclude with these thoughts. Mature love for God and for others has to be measured more by what we are giving than by what we are getting. Warm, fuzzy feelings sure are nice, but they are not a criterion of love for God or others. Loving God means obeying God and giving him prayer and worship. Loving our neighbor means helping them in whatever way we can. That's why in the Scriptures love is referred to as a commandment, because we don't always feel like praying or keeping the commandments; we do not always feel like helping our neighbor. Kathryn Hepburn said it so well: " You give because you love and cannot help giving. If you are very lucky, you may be loved back. That is delicious, but it does not necessarily happen." With God, however, God doesn't love us because we love him. He loved us first. The crucifix and the Eucharist demonstrate that. He just asks our love in return, which we offer each time we come to Mass. Amen.

All Saints
November 1, 2001

INTRODUCTION – (Rev 7:2-4,9-14, 1 John 3:1-3, Matt 5:1-12a) Our first reading is from the book of Revelation. The section just preceding today's passage described the end of the world. It described the sun becoming dark while the moon became red as blood and the great earthquake all over the earth. As people were trying to hide from all the terrible things that were happening, they asked the question "Who can survive?" Today's reading answers the question: those who have followed Christ faithfully, even through tribulation and persecution. Lest we think that 144,000 people are the only ones to be saved, the passage goes on to describe a crowd of people so large that they could not be numbered. Actually, the number 144,000 is symbolic of completion or perfection.

HOMILY – When we walk into St. Boniface church, we are surrounded by saints. And I don't mean just the saints here at Mass today. There are many holy people in our parish. However, I am talking about saints like the Blessed Virgin and St. Joseph, St. Rita, Sts. Martha and Mary with Jesus in the stained glass window, St. Teresa (aka, the Little Flower), all the apostles, St. John Vianney and St. Patrick in the back, St. Cecilia and St. Gregory the Great in the stained glass windows in the choir loft, St. Anthony, St. Boniface in the window. This is just a tiny sample of all the holy people the Church honors with the title "saint." There are thousands of others. My book of saints lists 7000. But who could count the number of holy people the Church has never honored as "saint?" That is that large crowd that the first reading tells us about, so large that no one could count them. There are many wonderful people I have known personally who are among them. And if the Church tried to honor all of them and assign them their own special feast day, it would take thousands of years to get through the list.

The Church today not only wants us to remember our relatives and friends who lived holy lives and who are now with God, but it also wants to remind us where we are headed if we live the way Jesus taught us to live. That is most important. If we read the lives of the saints we see that some were not always holy, but they realized they were doing wrong and they changed their ways. And we shouldn't wait until the last minute to change our ways either. I want to tell you an Irish story about a person who tried to wait until the last minute and it didn't work.

His name was Jack. He was smart, and he was lazy. He loved to drink too much whiskey and he loved to gamble. He never did a good thing for anyone his whole life. One Halloween night while he was at a bar, the devil showed up and told him it was time for him to die and the devil was going to take him to hell. Jack wasn't ready to die. He was pretty smart so he tried to figure out how to trick the devil. He told the devil "if you had all the power people say you do, you could turn yourself into a gold coin, but I'll bet you can't do it." The devil, being very proud, said "I can be anything I want." And he turned himself into a gold coin. Jack grabbed the coin and held it tight. It happened that Jack had a scar in the palm of his hand shaped like a cross and the devil is powerless in the presence of a cross. When the devil asked him to let him go, Jack told him he would only if the devil would give him another year to live. The devil agreed, so Jack opened his hand and let the devil go. Jack decided he would change his life during that year, but he was too busy drinking and gambling that he never got around to it. The next Halloween the devil showed up again. This time Jack challenged the devil to a game of dice. He agreed to go with the devil if he lost and if he won, he would have another year of life. The devil couldn't pass up the offer. Jack, being an expert gambler, won the toss and the devil lost again. Again, Jack said he would straighten out his life, but giving up his bad habits was too much effort and by the next Halloween he was no better. This time he really died and he found himself before St. Peter at heaven's gates. The devil didn't show up this time. He was still in hell, angry that Jack had tricked him twice. But St. Peter wouldn't let Jack in. He said he didn't belong there. But when Jack went to hell, even the devil didn't want him there either, he was so angry with him. "Where can I go," cried Jack. "I can't see in the dark." The devil tossed a burning coal into a pumpkin and ordered him to wander forever with only a pumpkin to light his path. From that day on he has been named Jack o' the lantern.

It's a fanciful story, but there are similar stories in the gospels where Jesus is telling us in all truthfulness we never know when our life will be ended and we always have to be prepared. We ask the Lord today to help us realize our dignity as God's children which St. John tells us about in today's second reading. And we ask our Lord to help us live our lives in such a way that we realize the purpose for which we were made, to live as God's children for all eternity with God in heaven.

All Souls
November 2, 2008

INTRODUCTION – (2 Maccabees 12: 43-46, Romans 5: 5-11, John 6: 37-40) Our first reading, from the book of Maccabees, comes from about 100 years before Christ. At that time in history the Greeks were the dominant power and they were trying to get the Jews to abandon their faith and follow the beliefs of the pagans. Those who would not give in were persecuted and put to death. The loyal Jews fought back. In one of their battles, many Jews were killed. As they were being buried, it was found that they had small statues of pagan gods attached to their garments. These Jews were loyal to their Jewish beliefs, but they had, to some extent, given in to paganism. Just in case those pagan gods were real, they were carrying with them statues of pagan gods to give them protection. Their leader, Judas Maccabeus, took up a collection to send to Jerusalem for sacrifices to be offered up to the Lord for those people. He believed their hearts were, in general, in the right place, but for the weakness in their faith they had to be forgiven. In this piece of history from 100 B.C., we can see the beginnings of the belief that our prayers can help those who have died, a belief that is still part of our faith.

HOMILY – Praying for our deceased relatives and friends is what our feast of All Souls is about today. However, I had the hardest time getting started with today's homily. I kept putting it off. It's not as if I do not believe in praying for friends and relatives who have died. I do it all the time and it has been a tradition in the Church from the beginning, and even before that as we heard in our first reading.

I think the difficulty I had in developing my homily comes from two sources. First, many people don't like to hear about death and what might come afterwards. We know we can't avoid it, but my sense is that many people believe that if they don't think about it, it won't happen, at least not for a long time. My suspicion is that my father was that way. I constantly tried to get him to make a will but he never did. As a CPA he would have known it was a good idea. I think making a will would have made the prospect of his own death too concrete and too real for him to deal with.

The second reason today's homily was hard was that I would have to talk about Purgatory. It's an idea that many Christians deny. I remember once I was helping a family prepare the liturgy for their deceased father and they insisted "absolutely no mention of Purgatory." It's as if it were a bad word. They wanted to think their father was perfect, I guess, and was already in heaven. Most of us would like to believe that our loved ones go straight to heaven when they die – period. If this were true, then they would not need our prayers. If they went to the other place, God forbid, our prayers would do them no good. The Church teaches, in every Mass we have for a person who died and in today's feast, that our prayers do help our relatives and friends who have left this world as they journey to eternal life.

Purgatory, among all the mysteries and beliefs of the Church is an extremely logical and comforting doctrine. It's logical if we ask ourselves how many of us think we will be perfect when we die. There may even be some who are perfect right now. I would ask them to identify themselves, but if they're perfect, they will also be too humble to do so. Even those who lived a good life may still have a little room for improvement, they may still not love God or others quite enough. That's where Purgatory comes in – it's an opportunity to grow into the most loving, most holy person we can possibly be. As a result we would then be filled with God's peace and joy and love to the fullest extent. Luther rejected the idea of Purgatory because of the abuse of indulgences at the time. Today, the concept of Purgatory has been rejected by many because of all the negative images of suffering and punishment that we grew up with. Actually, I think for the souls in Purgatory, happiness far outweighs the unhappiness. Their salvation is sure, they are more closely united with God than they had ever experienced before in their lives, they are on their way to the enjoyment of God's kingdom in the fullest possible way. But they're not there yet and that's the painful part.

If you read the book, "The Five People You Meet in Heaven," I think you get a good, practical image of Purgatory. It's not a religious book, it's very entertaining and it pictured for me what Purgatory might be like as we work out issues, regrets, hurts, conflicts, etc., that we might take with us when we die.

To demonstrate that Purgatory makes so much sense, I think that those who deny Purgatory have had to find a substitute for it in their thinking about the next life. For many that substitute is reincarnation. In reincarnation a person supposedly keeps working for greater and greater purity and holiness until they are ready to be perfectly one with God. However, reincarnation comes from Hinduism. Actually a Hindu does not look forward to reincarnation because they don't want to have to pass through this world of pain and suffering one more time. I suspect the notion of reincarnation has been adopted by many Westerners, even Christians, because it fits our culture of "buy now, pay later." They figure they can live any way they want and can postpone having to pay any consequences. Our faith tells us, "now is the acceptable time, now is the day of salvation." God gives us what we need in this life to help us know him and serve him in this life. If we do not do it perfectly, Purgatory is there to finish the job. Today, we renew our faith in life after death. Today too we renew our belief in the power of prayer to help our loved ones, even those who are no longer among us, for in Christ they are still one with us. With Christ our great high priest, we offer now the greatest prayer there is, the Eucharist.

31st Sunday in Ordinary Time
November 3, 2002

INTRODUCTION – (Malachi 1:14b-2:2b, 8-10, 1 Thessalonians 2:7b-9, 13, Matthew 23:1-12) Malachi was a real fire and brimstone prophet who lived about 400 years before Christ. He didn't write much, but what he wrote had a real punch. As the book of Malachi begins, he condemns the priests of his day for offering sacrifices unworthy of God, animals that were blind, lame and sick – the kind of animals the owner would have gotten rid of anyway. He said offer that to your governor and see if he would be pleased. Probably the one who made the offering also handed the priest a little bribe to sacrifice the sick animal, since the law commanded only perfect offerings were to be used in sacrifice. Also, the priests were causing people to sin by not giving true teachings. They told people things such as "everyone who does evil is good in the sight of the Lord, and he delights in them." Our first reading chastises these unfaithful priests, but it moves on to admonish the people who were unfaithful to God's covenant through sins of adultery, dishonesty and injustice.

HOMILY – If you think that our readings today are readings that we religious leaders need to reflect on, you are right. But in some ways, they contain lessons for anyone who calls himself or herself a Christian.

My homily today consists of two or three different thoughts that occurred to me as I read today's scriptures. Jesus in the gospel is condemning phoniness. One of my friends who is a truly spiritual person said to me the other day that someone told her she was a phony. She felt hurt by the comment. I told her we're all phonies to some extent in that we all fail at times to live up to our ideals, our values and our principles. The important thing is that we're honest with ourselves, that we recognize when we're being phony and make every effort to be better. Part of being honest means being open to feedback others give us about ourselves, no matter who says it or whether we like it or not. Whenever a person says something to me that hurts, I try to examine it to see if there is any truth in what was said and if there was, I try to benefit from it. Jesus, while he condemned the Pharisees and scribes for their phoniness, told the people they should follow what they say, because the scribes and Pharisees were speaking truth as they taught God's word, even though they were not living it.

Sometimes we have to teach others what's right or wrong, while we're not so perfect ourselves. But we have to realize we teach not only by what we say. I heard a story the other day about a father who punished one of his children for smoking and using bad language. But he smoked and used bad language himself. He was right in trying to guide his child correctly, but he will probably not be very effective. Children learn more from what they see than from what they hear.

On a slightly different topic: one of the frequent excuses people use who do not go to church is that they don't want to be with all those phonies. Why should a person deprive themselves of the graces of the Mass because of what they judge someone else to be or to do? I have talked to people who have quit going to church since the scandal of priest sexual abuse. There is no excuse for what some priests have done, but that doesn't mean all priests are bad, or that going to church now has no value.

On the other hand, we have to keep remembering that any of us who call ourselves Christians can lead people toward Christ or away from him by our lives. Mahatma Gandhi put it very forcefully when he said: "I like your Christ, but I don't like you Christians because you Christians are so unlike your Christ." For better or for worse it's not just priests but all of us who show the face of Christ to others.

Another idea I would like to consider is Jesus statement "call no man 'father'." You know sometimes Jesus sometimes uses figurative language to make a point. If Jesus intended us to take him literally we could not refer to our own father as "father." Nor should the gospels refer to anyone as being the father of anyone else.

So when Jesus said "you have but one Father in heaven" it reminds us who is the origin of all life and it reminds all of us that, although we may have a certain amount of authority over others, we too are under authority ourselves, under the authority of God.

We have to know the scriptures well to know what Jesus wants us to take literally and what not. We know for certain he does want us to take literally his words about the Eucharist: "This is my body " and "this is my blood." As we celebrate this sacrament that Christ gave us, we admit we are not perfect and that we are sinners, and we ask the Lord to help us in uniting us with himself to better live up to what he expects of us. Amen.

Dedication of St. John Lateran
November 9, 2008

INTRODUCTION – (Ezekiel 47:1-2,8-9,12, 1 Corinthians 3:9c-11,16-17, John 2:13-22) The celebration of the dedication of the Church of St. John Lateran in Rome is a universal feast of the Church. It is the oldest Catholic Church in Rome and it is the Cathedral Church of the Holy Father. Actually the popes lived there for 1000 years and it is still considered the Pope's cathedral. In a sense it symbolizes all existing churches in the world today.

Our first reading is a vision of the prophet Ezekiel who had lots of visions and recorded them. At the time this vision took place, Jerusalem and its Temple had been destroyed by the Babylonians. The prophet sees that one day the city would be restored and the temple would be rebuilt. It is an idealized temple he sees. There is a stream of water flowing from the temple, flowing east and south toward the desert of the Arabah and into the

Dead Sea. The water in the Dead Sea is seven times more salty than the ocean and nothing can live in it. In Ezekiel's vision, however, the water that flows from the temple gives life to everything it comes in contact with and even makes the Dead Sea into fresh water. The meaning is that what flows from God's house, prayer and sacrifice and worship is life giving. The book of Revelations takes up this image, for the vision is still waiting to be fulfilled.

HOMILY – Buildings are important not just to keep us warm and dry. They are important for many, many reasons. Winston Churchill said it so clearly when London had to be rebuilt after the World War II. "We shape our buildings then our buildings shape our lives." Today we celebrate the dedication of a church building. A church building is a holy place, a place where God's people gather for prayer and worship and sacrifice. Jesus' reaction to the abuses in the Temple shows us God's house should be treated as a holy place.

But a church building is important not just because God is there but because we are. A church building is called a church only because it is where the Church gathers and prays and celebrates God's saving love. Without the gathering of God's people, it would not be a church, even if it were the most beautiful building ever built. Today's celebration reminds us the Church is first and foremost the community of God's people, for the Church existed for almost 300 years before the first building was built. Before then the Church met in people's homes or during times of persecution they met in catacombs in order to pray and celebrate the Eucharist. Notice that gathering together was so important that the early Christians would risk their lives in order to do so. When Constantine became emperor he issued the edict of toleration thus ending the persecution. It was he who built St. John Lateran. So today's commemoration of St. John Lateran is a feast worth celebrating; it's also a feast reminding us that Church is more than a place to go. It is all of us who gather together here or anywhere else God's people come together to pray.

So many people today claim to belong to a Church, but they are seldom there. I think they deceive themselves to say they belong to a Church unless they belong to the gathering of God's people. That's what Church really is. In the second reading St. Paul says, "You are God's building." Those who are physically unable to be part of the gathering because of sickness or infirmity are still connected with us through the Eucharist our Communion ministers take to them each week. Belonging to a Church is more than having your name on a church's roster or in the church's computer. Being part of a church involves more than simply believing in Christ. St. James tells us the devils also believe...and tremble with fear. (James 2,19) Later on in his letter, Paul uses another example to show that following Christ means being part of a community of believers. He tells us we are all members of Christ's body and we need to be united and work together as one. Certainly, coming together in prayer and worship is an expression of our oneness in Christ. (It would be nice if we showed this oneness by coming closer to the altar when we come to pray and not spread all over church. But that's another issue.)

Sometimes it's hard to be part of a community each week. We can all find reasons why we're too busy to get to church. We live in a society that promotes the attitude that we can make up our own rules. When we're part of a community, not everyone is as perfect as we are. There are scandals and there is hypocrisy in the Church.

I always remind people of the statement by Fr. Greeley: "If you ever find a perfect church, by all means join it. Just know that once you join it, it will no longer be perfect." The Church has been scarred with failures and sins from the time Judas betrayed Christ and Peter denied him. But Christ hasn't given up on his Church and continues to be with us and to call us to holiness. He promised he will be with us always until the end of time. We continue to offer our prayers asking God to bless us as his people gathered in faith. Amen.

32nd Sunday in Ordinary Time
November 10, 2002

HOMILY – (Wisdom 6:12-16, 1 Thessalonians 4:13-18, Matthew 25:1-13) Did you notice that this parable was all about being prepared, but at the end Jesus said "Stay awake?" That is a curious conclusion after telling us about 10 people who didn't stay awake, but in spite of that, half of them were rewarded for thinking ahead. Why do you think Jesus ended with this directive "Stay awake?" I'll tell you why later.

This past Monday (Nov. 4) was the feast of St. Charles Borromeo. There is a lovely story told about him. One evening he was playing cards with a few of his friends and the subject got around to death and dying. What would you do, it was asked, if all of a sudden it were revealed that you were going to die this very night? One person said: "I'd run off to confession." Another said "I'd get down on my knees and pray." Someone else said: "I would find my lawyer and make sure my will was in good order." Charles kept silent, continuing to look at his cards. Eventually, remarking on his lack of response, his friends asked him what he would do. "I'd continue to play cards," was his reply.

He was ready at any time. I guess that's why Charles Borromeo was a saint. That's the way our Lord tells us we should be in today's gospel. Today's parable is one that makes us uncomfortable. We all prefer parables like the prodigal son who came home after his wild affair and the father threw his arms around him to welcome him and killed the fatted calf to celebrate. But we sometimes over look the part of that parable that says that before his reunion with his father the boy had to come to his senses and decide to return home.

In today's parable we would rather our Lord had told us the master of the house said to the late comers "Come on in." But he didn't. They missed out because they weren't prepared. God is always ready to welcome us back if we are willing to change our ways, but our Lord warns us in today's parable we never know when time will run out for us.

When we hear today's parable, we think the ones who brought enough oil were being very selfish. But instead of thinking of 10 bridesmaids, lets think of 10 students going in to class and the teacher is about to have a pop quiz. Five of the students had been studying all along and knew the material. The other five had been partying and cutting class or sleeping through the lectures. The five prepared students couldn't suddenly transmit their knowledge to the other five. The oil represents something intangible. It represents for example a relationship with God which must be personally developed and which cannot just be given to someone else any more than any close relationship can. Someone once wrote an article entitled: God has no Grandchildren. We either have a relationship with God as son or daughter or we do not. We cannot have a relationship with God because someone else we know or we're related to does. We have to have it for ourselves.

The oil could stand for character. A person cannot take someone else's character and make it their own. They have to acquire it for themselves. It could stand for the good works we have done. It could stand for grace which God gives us as we serve him and love him. What our Lord is telling us is that whatever will get us into the party is intangible, something each of us has to acquire for ourselves.

I heard an interesting story about an architect who worked for a company for most of his adult life. One day the company gave him a $1,000,000 budget and commissioned him to build a beautiful house. He was to use the best materials in the building. He decided he would be out of the business in a short time, so although the house looked wonderful, he used poor materials and did a job that was substandard in many ways. When he finished the job, the company told him in appreciation for his many years of service they were giving him that house. We are right now, whether we know it or not, building our own future.

Now I'm not telling you anything you don't already know. We all know death is going to catch up with us sometime and we don't know when that time will be. And I think this is what our Lord means by telling us to "stay awake." What this really means is to stay aware, because if we remain aware of how fragile life is, how suddenly it might come to an end for any of us, we will be prepared.

Our relationship with God is as practical as so many other things in life. We can't run our car without putting gas in the tank. We can't pass a test if we don't have the required knowledge. We can't write a check and not have it bounce if we don't have the money in the bank. We can't stay healthy if we don't eat. There are certain things in life that require something of us if we want the desirable results. Heaven's like that. It's not a geographical place where God decides he's going to put us if we're good or keep us out of if we're bad. It's essentially a state of happiness, a state of being in love with an infinite lover – a state that we have to open our hearts to right now. And how do we open our hearts to that love? The answer is pretty simple. Jesus tells us if you love me you will keep my commandments. He tells us what we do to others we do to him. He tells us not to have strange gods before him. And whatever puts him in second place in our lives is a false god for us. In other words we must obey him, give him the worship we owe him and love him and love each other. That's not too hard. And that's part of the reason why we're here today.

33rd Sunday in Ordinary Time
November 16, 2008

HOMILY – (Proverbs 31: 10-13,19-20,30-31, 1 Thessalonians 5: 1-6, Matthew 25: 14-30) With the economy the way it is today, there is the temptation to be like the man in today's gospel and bury whatever we might have left of our assets in some safe place. I remain hopeful that what I read about things getting better will be correct. Our story, however, is not about how we should invest our money but how to invest our lives. The only safe investment is to invest our lives in God and to live our faith as best we can.

When we hear the word talent, we automatically think of some special gift, like writing poetry or singing or drawing or playing sports. In today's parable the talents the master gave his servants were indeed special gifts, but in the vocabulary of the ancients it referred to a specific weight – 60 to 80 pounds of gold or silver. Our word "talent" comes from the Greek word τάλαντον.

Jesus doesn't tell us what the metal was, but it would indeed have been a special gift.

The third man, the man with the one talent, said he was too afraid of his boss to risk investing it. The thought struck me that maybe the other two had just as much fear of their master and that's what motivated them to do something with the talents they had been given. Fear is not always bad. Sometimes it motivates us to action rather than immobilize us. That idea might be an interesting topic for some other time.

What I want to tell you today is what you already know. If we work hard, we will be more likely to succeed in life than if we don't! Outside circumstances (which we call luck: good or bad) can affect our efforts, but for the most part we get out of life what we put into it. That's a no-brainer.

Jesus is telling us that our eternal happiness works the same way. We will get out of our spiritual life what we put into it. Too many people today hear only what they want to hear in the gospel. They enjoy hearing all about God's mercy and love, but they tend to ignore the places where Jesus tells us about our responsibilities. Today's parable tells us heaven is not a freebie and it's not automatic. If it were, why did Jesus need to come to us in the first place. Why did he teach us how to live and stress the importance of prayer and doing good works? Grace is indeed a gift, but if we don't use the graces and gifts and love God offers us, we will lose them. It's just like any talent we can think of – if we don't use it, it does us no good to have it. God can't save us without our cooperation. If his parable doesn't tell us that, it doesn't tell us anything.

We've all put time and energy into something and been disappointed. It may have been an investment, it may have been a relationship, it may have been anything at all. When that happens we may shy away from risking disappointment again. But even though the world can disappoint us, God will not.

Faith in our Lord will not disappoint, but it will not bring payoffs every time we pray or do something good. If that were to happen, faith would be unnecessary. The reason we need faith is because we are not always immediately blessed for some good thing we do. When we are, that's great. When we're not, we just have to trust that God will not let us down in the end. Notice in the parable, the servants who invested their gift and increased its value received a reward that greatly outweighed the original gift, but they didn't receive it until the master returned. The kingdom of heaven will be greater than anything we can imagine and will far outweigh any good thing we are able to do, but we have to wait for it with faith and hope.

Our Mass reminds us of how we have been blessed, it reminds us of our responsibilities, it encourages us to remain faithful. It not only encourages us, the Mass is the greatest prayer we have. As a prayer it helps us to use well the gifts God has given us, especially the gift of his grace. Amen.

Christ the King
November 23, 2008

INTRODUCTION – (Ezekiel 34:11-12.15-17; 1 Corinthians 15: 20-26,28; Matthew 25:31-46) Today we honor Christ as our King. Our scripture readings do not picture him as a typical king. In our first reading Ezekiel, the prophet, pictures God as a shepherd. God is distressed with the shepherds of his people; i.e., the kings and religious leaders. They led God's people away from

God and to eventual disaster when the Babylonians invaded. God said he would lead them rightly. We see this prophecy perfectly fulfilled in Jesus. In our second reading St. Paul is writing on the topic of the resurrection. Paul tells us the risen Jesus will reign until all evil in the world is destroyed, even death, and then he will turn the kingdom over to the Father. In the gospel Jesus is pictured as a judge, a judge who judges us on how we behave toward the lowly and the poor. Thus we have three images of Christ the King: a shepherd, the risen Lord and the judge of all nations.

HOMILY – This past week I was asked to speak to the students in one of our local high schools. The topic was Judaism. It was an interesting experience being back in the classroom. Unfortunately they were not as excited about Jewish history as I am. I put half the students to sleep and said to the teacher as I was leaving, "I'm sorry I put many of your students to sleep." He said, "that's all right. I do it every day as well." In reading about Judaism I came across a story about two rabbis who were walking together. They were approached by a non-believer who was interested in perhaps joining the Jewish religion. He said to the two rabbis, "can you teach me all I need to know about being a Jew while I stand on one foot?" The one rabbi thought it was a trivial and irreverent question and hit him with his cane for asking it. The other rabbi said it can be done. He told him this is the essence of the law: "Do not do unto others what you would not have them do unto you." He added, "the rest is commentary, but study the rest as well."

The second rabbi was very wise in getting to the heart of the matter. There is One even wiser who told us that the essence of the law is really in two parts: first of all we must love God with our whole heart and soul and mind and strength and, secondly, love our neighbor as ourselves.

Jesus' parable today focuses on the second great commandment to love one another as we love ourselves. It implies, of course, that we love ourselves. If you hate yourself, then don't love me like you love yourself.

Most Christians have pretty much absorbed the message of today's gospel. And probably most Christians will be surprised at the final judgment when Jesus tells us, "I was hungry and you gave me to eat, etc." Most of us do it simply because we know we've been blessed more than we deserve and helping someone less fortunate is what we know Christ would have us do. There are many in the world who do not even know Christ and who are non-believers, and they too are kind to others and to the less fortunate just because they know it's the right thing to do. They will really be surprised when Christ tells them, "I was hungry and you gave me to eat."

While we do good for others, the lesson in today's gospel, we can't forget the first commandment Jesus gave us: we must love God with our whole heart and soul and mind and strength. Loving God must include prayer and worship. If Jesus didn't mention the importance of prayer and worship in today's parable of the last judgment, it was because Jesus was talking to Jews who observed the Sabbath and went to synagogue every week. Jesus himself did so. It was part of their culture. Additionally a good Jew would pray two or three times a day as well as observe all the feast days. So Jesus did not need to remind them of their obligations to God, nor did St. Matthew when he wrote this passage for he was writing to Christians who at the time risked their lives to come together for the Eucharist on the Lord's day. Jesus, and Matthew who recorded Jesus' parable, were stressing to church-going people that just going to church is not enough to be a good Christian.

Christ our king is not an elected person whom we can vote out of office if we don't like what he tells us. When we honor him as our king, we commit ourselves to following him faithfully – the only path that will lead to his kingdom. We have a celebration of thanksgiving this week, but our thanks should be offered more than once a year. It should be offered daily and especially weekly in the perfect offering of thanksgiving, the Eucharist. So let us continue honoring our king who shepherds us and blesses us and will some day expect us to account for how we have lived in his love and grace. Amen.

A Priest Is a Gift from God

by Rita Ring

How to Become a
Shepherd of Christ Associate

The Shepherds of Christ has prayer chapters all over the world praying for the priests, the Church and the world. These prayers that Father Carter compiled in the summer of 1994 began this worldwide network of prayer. Currently the prayers are in eight languages with the Church's Imprimatur. Fr. Carter had the approval of his Jesuit provincial for this movement, writing the Newsletter every 2 months for 6 1/2 years. After his death, and with his direction, we in the Shepherds of Christ circulated the Priestly Newsletter Book II to 95,000 priests with other writings. We have prayed daily for the priests, the Church, and the world since 1994. Associates are called to join prayer Chapters and help us circulate this newsletter centered on spreading devotion to the Sacred Heart and Immaculate Heart and helping to renew the Church through greater holiness. Please form a Prayer Chapter & order a Prayer Manual.

Apostles of the Eucharistic Heart of Jesus

The Shepherds of Christ have people dedicated to spending two hours weekly before the Blessed Sacrament in the Tabernacle. They pray for the following intentions:

1) For the spread of the devotion to the Hearts of Jesus and Mary culminating in the reign of the Sacred Heart and the triumph of the Immaculate Heart.
2) For the Pope.
3) For all bishops of the world.
4) For all priests.
5) For all sisters and brothers in religious life.
6) For all members of the Shepherds of Christ Movement, and for the spread of this movement to the world.
7) For all members of the Catholic Church.
8) For all members of the human family.
9) For all souls in purgatory.

This movement, *Apostles of the Eucharistic Heart of Jesus*, was began with Fr. Carter. Please inquire. Shepherds of Christ Ministries P.O. Box 627, China, Indiana 47250 USA or 1-888-211-3041 or info@sofc.org

Prayer for Union with Jesus

Come to me, Lord, and possess my soul. Come into my heart and permeate my soul. Help me to sit in silence with You and let You work in my heart.

I am Yours to possess.  I am Yours to use. I want to be selfless and only exist in You. Help me to spoon out all that is me and be an empty vessel ready to be filled by You. Help me to die to myself and live only for You. Use me as You will. Let me never draw my attention back to myself. I only want to operate as You do, dwelling within me.

I am Yours, Lord. I want to have my life in You. I want to do the will of the Father. Give me the strength to put aside the world and let You operate my very being. Help me to act as You desire. Strengthen me against the distractions of the devil to take me from Your work.

When I worry, I have taken my focus off of You and placed it on myself. Help me not to give in to the promptings of others to change what in my heart You are making very clear to me. I worship You, I adore You and I love You. Come and dwell in me now.

Prayer Before the
Holy Sacrifice of the Mass

Let me be a holy sacrifice and unite with God in the sacrament of His greatest love.

I want to be one in Him in this act of love, where He gives Himself to me and I give myself as a sacrifice to Him. Let me be a holy sacrifice as I become one with Him in this my act of greatest love to Him.

Let me unite with Him more, that I may more deeply love Him. May I help make reparation to His adorable Heart and the heart of His Mother, Mary. With greatest love, I offer myself to You and pray that You will accept my sacrifice of greatest love. I give myself to You and unite in Your gift of Yourself to me. Come and possess my soul.

Cleanse me, strengthen me, heal me. Dear Holy Spirit act in the heart of Mary to make me more and more like Jesus.

Father, I offer this my sacrifice, myself united to Jesus in the Holy Spirit to You. Help me to love God more deeply in this act of my greatest love.

Give me the grace to grow in my knowledge, love and service of You and for this to be my greatest participation in the Mass. Give me the greatest graces to love You so deeply in this Mass, You who are so worthy of my love.

Father Carter requested
that these be prayed in prayer
chapters all over the world.

Shepherds of Christ

Prayers

Shepherds of Christ Associates

PRAYER MANUAL

Shepherds of Christ Publications
China, Indiana

Imprimi Potest: Rev. Bradley M. Schaeffer, S.J.
          Provincial
          Chicago Province, The Society of Jesus
    Imprimatur: Most Rev. Carl K. Moeddel
          Auxiliary Bishop
          Archdiocese of Cincinnati

The Shepherds of Christ Associates Prayer Manual is published by
Shepherds of Christ Publications, an arm of Shepherds of Christ Ministries,
P.O. Box 627 China, Indiana 47250 USA.

    Founder, Shepherds of Christ Ministries:
    Father Edward J. Carter, S.J.

    For more information contact:
    Shepherds of Christ Associates
    P.O. Box 627
    China, Indiana 47250- USA
    Tel. 812-273-8405
    Toll Free: 1-888-211-3041
    Fax 812-273-3182

Chapter Meeting
Prayer Format

The prayer format below should be followed at chapter meetings of *Shepherds of Christ Associates*. All prayers, not just those said specifically for priests, should include the intention of praying for all the needs of priests the world over.

1. **Hymns.** Hymns may be sung at any point of the prayer part of the meeting.

2. **Holy Spirit Prayer.** Come, Holy Spirit, almighty Sanctifier, God of love, who filled the Virgin Mary with grace, who wonderfully changed the hearts of the apostles, who endowed all Your martyrs with miraculous courage, come and sanctify us. Enlighten our minds, strengthen our wills, purify our consciences, rectify our judgment, set our hearts on fire, and preserve us from the misfortunes of resisting Your inspirations. Amen.

3. **The Rosary.**

4. **Salve Regina.** "Hail Holy Queen, Mother of mercy, our life, our sweetness, and our hope. To you do we cry, poor banished children of Eve. To you do we send up our sighs, our mourning, our weeping in this vale of tears. Turn, then, most gracious advocate, your eyes of mercy toward us and after this, our exile, show unto us the blessed fruit of your womb, Jesus, O clement, O loving, O sweet Virgin Mary. Amen."

5. **The Memorare.** "Remember, O most gracious Virgin Mary, that never was it known that anyone who fled to your protection, implored your help, or sought your intercession was left unaided. Inspired by this confidence, I fly unto you, O Virgin of virgins, my Mother. To you I come, before you I stand, sinful and

sorrowful. O Mother of the Word Incarnate, despise not my petitions, but, in your mercy, hear and answer me. Amen."

6. **Seven Hail Marys in honor of the Seven Sorrows of Mary.** Mary has promised very special graces to those who do this on a daily basis. Included in the promises of Our Lady for those who practice this devotion is her pledge to give special assistance at the hour of death, including the sight of her face. The seven sorrows are:

(1) The first sorrow: the prophecy of Simeon (Hail Mary).

(2) The second sorrow: the flight into Egypt (Hail Mary).

(3) The third sorrow: the loss of the Child Jesus in the temple (Hail Mary).

(4) The fourth sorrow: Jesus and Mary meet on the way to the cross (Hail Mary).

(5) The fifth sorrow: Jesus dies on the cross (Hail Mary).

(6) The sixth sorrow: Jesus is taken down from the cross and laid in Mary's arms (Hail Mary).

(7) The seventh sorrow: the burial of Jesus (Hail Mary).

7. **Litany of the Blessed Virgin Mary.**
Lord, have mercy on us.
Christ, have mercy on us.
Lord, have mercy on us. Christ, hear us.
Christ, graciously hear us.
God, the Father of heaven, *have mercy on us.*
God, the Son, Redeemer of the world,
have mercy on us.
God, the Holy Spirit, *have mercy on us.*
Holy Trinity, one God, *have mercy on us.*
Holy Mary, *pray for us* (repeat after each invocation).

Holy Mother of God,
Holy Virgin of virgins,
Mother of Christ,
Mother of the Church,
Mother of divine grace,
Mother most pure,
Mother most chaste,
Mother inviolate,
Mother undefiled,
Mother most amiable,
Mother most admirable,
Mother of good counsel,
Mother of our Creator,
Mother of our Savior,
Virgin most prudent,
Virgin most venerable,
Virgin most renowned,
Virgin most powerful,
Virgin most merciful,
Virgin most faithful,
Mirror of justice,
Seat of wisdom,
Cause of our joy,
Spiritual vessel,
Vessel of honor,
Singular vessel of devotion,
Mystical rose,
Tower of David,
Tower of ivory,
House of gold,
Ark of the Covenant,
Gate of heaven,
Morning star,
Health of the sick,
Refuge of sinners,

Comforter of the afflicted,
Help of Christians,
Queen of angels,
Queen of patriarchs,
Queen of prophets,
Queen of apostles,
Queen of martyrs,
Queen of confessors,
Queen of virgins,
Queen of all saints,
Queen conceived without original sin,
Queen assumed into heaven,
Queen of the most holy rosary,
Queen of families,
Queen of peace,
Lamb of God, who take away the sins of the world,
  spare us, O Lord.
Lamb of God, who take away the sins of the world,
  graciously hear us, O Lord.
Lamb of God, who take away the sins of the world,
  have mercy on us.
Pray for us, O holy Mother of God,
  that we may be made worthy of the promises of
  Christ.

Let us pray: Grant, we beseech You, O Lord God, that we Your servants may enjoy perpetual health of mind and body and, by the glorious intercession of the blessed Mary, ever virgin, be delivered from present sorrow, and obtain eternal joy. Through Christ our Lord. Amen.

We fly to your patronage, O holy Mother of God. Despise not our petitions in our necessities, but deliver us always from all dangers, O glorious and blessed Virgin. Amen.

8. **Prayer to St. Joseph.** St. Joseph, guardian of Jesus and

chaste spouse of Mary, you passed your life in perfect fulfillment of duty. You supported the Holy Family of Nazareth with the work of your hands. Kindly protect those who trustingly turn to you. You know their aspirations, their hardships, their hopes; and they turn to you because they know you will understand and protect them. You too have known trial, labor, and weariness. But, even amid the worries of material life, your soul was filled with deep peace and sang out in true joy through intimacy with the Son of God entrusted to you, and with Mary, His tender Mother. Amen.

— *(Pope John XXIII)*

9. **Litany of the Sacred Heart, promises of the Sacred Heart.**

Lord, have mercy on us.
Christ, have mercy on us.
Lord, have mercy on us. Christ, hear us.
Christ, graciously hear us.
God the Father of heaven,
have mercy on us (repeat after each invocation).
God the Son, Redeemer of the world,
God the Holy Spirit,
Holy Trinity, one God,
Heart of Jesus, Son of the eternal Father,
Heart of Jesus, formed by the Holy Spirit in the womb of the Virgin Mother,
Heart of Jesus, substantially united to the Word of God,
Heart of Jesus, of infinite majesty,
Heart of Jesus, sacred temple of God,
Heart of Jesus, tabernacle of the Most High,
Heart of Jesus, house of God and gate of heaven,
Heart of Jesus, burning furnace of charity,
Heart of Jesus, abode of justice and love,
Heart of Jesus, full of goodness and love,
Heart of Jesus, abyss of all virtues,

Heart of Jesus, most worthy of all praise,
Heart of Jesus, king and center of all hearts,
Heart of Jesus, in whom are all the treasures of wisdom
and knowledge,
Heart of Jesus, in whom dwells the fullness of divinity,
Heart of Jesus, in whom the Father is well pleased,
Heart of Jesus, of whose fullness we have all
received,
Heart of Jesus, desire of the everlasting hills,
Heart of Jesus, patient and most merciful,
Heart of Jesus, enriching all who invoke You,
Heart of Jesus, fountain of life and holiness,
Heart of Jesus, propitiation for our sins,
Heart of Jesus, loaded down with opprobrium,
Heart of Jesus, bruised for our offenses,
Heart of Jesus, obedient even to death,
Heart of Jesus, pierced with a lance,
Heart of Jesus, source of all consolation,
Heart of Jesus, our life and reconciliation,
Heart of Jesus, victim of sin,
Heart of Jesus, salvation of those who hope in You,
Heart of Jesus, hope of those who die in You,
Heart of Jesus, delight of all the saints,
Lamb of God, Who take away the sins of the world,
spare us, O Lord.
Lamb of God, Who take away the sins of the world,
graciously hear us, O Lord.
Lamb of God, Who take away the sins of the world,
have mercy on us.
Jesus, meek and humble of heart,
make our hearts like unto Yours.

Let us pray: O almighty and eternal God, look upon
the Heart of Your dearly beloved Son and upon the praise
and satisfaction He offers You in behalf of sinners and,
being appeased, grant pardon to those who seek Your

mercy, in the name of the same Jesus Christ, Your Son, Who lives and reigns with You, in the unity of the Holy Spirit, world without end. Amen.

Promises of Our Lord to those devoted to His Sacred Heart (these should be read by the prayer leader):

(1) I will give them all the graces necessary in their state of life.

(2) I will establish peace in their homes.

(3) I will comfort them in all their afflictions.

(4) I will be their refuge during life and above all in death.

(5) I will bestow a large blessing on all their undertakings.

(6) Sinners shall find in My Heart the source and the infinite ocean of mercy.

(7) Tepid souls shall grow fervent.

(8) Fervent souls shall quickly mount to high perfection.

(9) I will bless every place where a picture of My Heart shall be set up and honored.

(10) I will give to priests the gift of touching the most hardened hearts.

(11) Those who promote this devotion shall have their names written in My Heart, never to be blotted out.

(12) I promise you in the excessive mercy of My Heart that My all-powerful love will grant to all those who communicate on the first Friday in nine consecutive months the grace of final penitence; they shall not die in My disgrace nor without receiving their sacraments; My divine Heart shall be their safe refuge in this last moment.

10. **Prayer for Priests.** "Lord Jesus, Chief Shepherd of the Flock, we pray that in the great love and mercy of Your Sacred Heart You attend to all the needs of Your priest-shepherds throughout the world. We ask that You draw

back to Your Heart all those priests who have seriously strayed from Your path, that You rekindle the desire for holiness in the hearts of those priests who have become lukewarm, and that You continue to give Your fervent priests the desire for the highest holiness. United with Your Heart and Mary's Heart, we ask that You take this petition to Your heavenly Father in the unity of the Holy Spirit. Amen."

11. **Prayer for all members of the Shepherds of Christ Associates.** "Dear Jesus, we ask Your special blessings on all members of Shepherds of Christ Associates. Continue to enlighten them regarding the very special privilege and responsibility you have given them as members of Your movement, Shepherds of Christ Associates. Draw them ever closer to Your Heart and to Your Mother's Heart. Allow them to more and more realize the great and special love of Your Hearts for each of them as unique individuals. Give them the grace to respond to Your love and Mary's love with an increased love of their own. As they dwell in Your Heart and Mary's Heart, abundantly care for all their needs and those of their loved ones. We make our prayer through You to the Father, in the Holy Spirit, with Mary our Mother at our side. Amen."

12. **Prayer for the spiritual and financial success of the priestly newsletter.** "Father, we ask Your special blessings upon the priestly newsletter, Shepherds of Christ. We ask that You open the priest-readers to the graces You wish to give them through this chosen instrument of Your Son. We also ask that You provide for the financial needs of the newsletter and the Shepherds of Christ Associates. We make our prayer through Jesus, in the Holy Spirit, with Mary at our side. Amen."

13. Prayer for all members of the human family.
"Heavenly Father, we ask Your blessings on all Your children the world over. Attend to all their needs. We ask Your special assistance for all those marginalized people, all those who are so neglected and forgotten. United with our Mother Mary, we make this petition to You through Jesus and in the Holy Spirit. Amen."

14. Prayer to St. Michael and our Guardian Angels:
"St. Michael the Archangel, defend us in battle. Be our safeguard against the wickedness and snares of the devil. May God rebuke him, we humbly pray, and do thou, O prince of the heavenly hosts, by the power of God, cast into hell Satan and all the other evil spirits who prowl about the world seeking the ruin of souls. Amen."

"Angel of God, my guardian dear, to whom God's love commits me here, ever this day be at my side, to light and guard, to rule and guide. Amen."

15. Pause for silent, personal prayer. This should last at least five minutes.

16. Act of consecration to the Sacred Heart of Jesus and the Immaculate Heart of Mary.

"Lord Jesus, Chief Shepherd of the flock, I consecrate myself to Your most Sacred Heart. From Your pierced Heart the Church was born, the Church You have called me, as a member of Shepherds of Christ Associates, to serve in a most special way. You reveal Your Heart as a symbol of Your love in all its aspects, including Your most special love for me, whom You have chosen as Your companion in this most important work. Help me to always love You in return. Help me to give myself entirely to You. Help me always to pour out my life in love of God and neighbor! Heart of Jesus, I place my trust in You!

"Dear Blessed Virgin Mary, I consecrate myself to your maternal and Immaculate Heart, this Heart which is symbol of your life of love. You are the Mother of my Savior. You are also my Mother. You love me with a most special love as a member of Shepherds of Christ Associates, a movement created by your Son as a powerful instrument for the renewal of the Church and the world. In a return of love, I give myself entirely to your motherly love and protection. You followed Jesus perfectly. You are His first and perfect disciple. Teach me to imitate you in the putting on of Christ. Be my motherly intercessor so that, through your Immaculate Heart, I may be guided to an ever closer union with the pierced Heart of Jesus, Chief Shepherd of the flock."

17.**Daily Prayers.** All members should say the Holy Spirit prayer daily and make the act of consecration daily. They should also pray the rosary each day. They are encouraged to use the other above prayers as time allows.

Other great books
published
by
Shepherds of Christ
Publications

To order any of the following materials please contact us by mail, phone, fax, email or the Internet:

Shepherds of Christ Publications
P.O. Box 627
China, Indiana 47250 USA

Toll free USA: (888) 211-3041
Tel: (812) 273-8405   Fax: (812) 273-3182
Email: info@sofc.org   http://www.sofc.org

Please contact us for *Prayer Manuals* or to begin a Prayer Chapter to pray for the priests, the Church and the world.

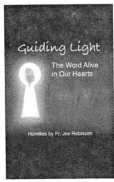

C1. *The Word Alive in Our Hearts - Partial Cycle A* $5
C2. *Focusing on the Word - Complete Cycle B* $10
C3. *Feed My Soul - Complete Cycle C* $10
C4. *Guiding Light - Complete Cycle A (this book)* $10

Guiding Light homily series by the Reverend Joe Robinson given at St. Boniface Church in Cincinnati, Ohio. It is a tremendous honor Fr. Joe has allowed us to share these great gifts with you – for greater holiness and knowing more and more about God.

B8.   Mass Book, by Rita Ring: Many of the entries in the Priestly Newsletter Volume II from a spiritual journal came from this book. These entries are to help people to be more deeply united to God in the Mass. This book is available in English and Spanish with the Church's *Imprimatur.* $12

BN4.   *Response to God's Love* by Fr. Edward J. Carter, S.J. In this book Fr. Carter speaks of God as the ultimate mystery. We can meditate on the interior life of the Trinity. Fr. Carter tells us about our uniqueness in the Father's Plan for us, how the individual Christian, the Church and the world are in the state of becoming. *Imprimatur.* $10

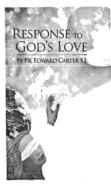

BN3. *Shepherds of Christ - Volume 3* by Fr. Edward J. Carter, S.J. Contains Newsletter Issues 1 through 4 of 2000 including Fr. Carter's tremendous *Overview of the Spiritual Life* $10

BN2. *Shepherds of Christ - Volume 2:* by Fr. Edward J. Carter, S.J. Contains issues 13-29 of the newsletter (September/October 1996 - Issue 5, 1999) $15

BN1. *Shepherds of Christ - Selected Writings on Spirituality for all People* as Published in Shepherds of Christ Newsletter for Priests. Contains 12 issues of the newsletter from July/August 1994 to May/June 1996. $15

B7. *Rosary Meditations for Parents and Children*, by Rita Ring, Short Meditations for both parents and children to be used when praying the rosary. These meditations will help all to know the lives of Jesus and Mary alive in their Hearts. Available in both English and Spanish with the Church's *Imprimatur.* $10

Shepherds of Christ Ministries

<u>Send Order To:</u>
Shepherds of Christ Ministries
P.O. Box 627
China, Indiana 47250 USA

Order Form

	<u>Qty</u>	<u>Total $</u>
P1. Prayer Manuals	___	___
C1. The Word Alive in Our Hearts ($5)	___	___
C2. Focusing on the Word - Cycle B ($10)	___	___
C3. Feed My Soul - Cycle C ($10)	___	___
C4. Guiding Light - Cycle A ($10)	___	___
B8. Mass Book ($12)	___	___
BN4. Response to God's Love ($10)	___	___
BN3. Shepherds of Christ - Volume 3 ($10)	___	___
BN2. Shepherds of Christ - Volume 2 ($15)	___	___
BN1. Shepherds of Christ - Volume 1 ($15)	___	___
B7. Rosary Meditations for Parents and Children ($10)	___	___
Totals:	___	___

Name: _____

Address: _____

City: _____ State: _____ Zip: _____

For More Information Call Toll free USA: 1-888-211-3041